WORLD HISTORY SERIES

The Louisiana Purchase

Titles in the World History Series

WORLD HISTORY ■ ■ ■

The Louisiana Purchase

by
James A. Corrick

Lucent Books, P.O. Box 289011, San Diego, CA 92198-9011

On Cover: A painting depicting the ceremony of land transfer for the Louisiana Purchase in 1804.

For Tom, Laurie, Betsy, and Mary—the Corricks of Idaho

Library of Congress Cataloging-in-Publication Data

Corrick, James A.
  The Louisiana Purchase / by James A Corrick.
    p. cm. — (World history series)
Includes bibliographical references and index.
Summary: Examines the Louisiana Purchase, discussing the negotiation of the treaty with France, the formation of Louisiana, taking possession of the land, and the exploration, growth, and settlement of the territory.
  ISBN 1-56006-637-7 (alk. paper)
  1. Louisiana Purchase—Juvenile literature. [1. Louisiana Purchase.] I. Title. II. Series.
  E333 .C76 2001
    973.4'6—dc21
                                                        00-009156
                                                        CIP

Contents

Foreword

Each year on the first day of school, nearly every history teacher faces the task of explaining why his or her students should study history. One logical answer to this question is that exploring what happened in our past explains how the things we often take for granted—our customs, ideas, and institutions—came to be. As statesman and historian Winston Churchill put it, "Every nation or group of nations has its own tale to tell. Knowledge of the trials and struggles is necessary to all who would comprehend the problems, perils, challenges, and opportunities which confront us today." Thus, a study of history puts modern ideas and institutions in perspective. For example, though the founders of the United States were talented and creative thinkers, they clearly did not invent the concept of democracy. Instead, they adapted some democratic ideas that had originated in ancient Greece and with which the Romans, the British, and others had experimented. An exploration of these cultures, then, reveals their very real connection to us through institutions that continue to shape our daily lives.

Another reason often given for studying history is the idea that lessons exist in the past from which contemporary societies can benefit and learn. This idea, although controversial, has always been an intriguing one for historians. Those who agree that society can benefit from the past often quote philosopher George Santayana's famous statement, "Those who cannot remember the past are condemned to repeat it." Historians who subscribe to Santayana's philosophy believe that, for example, studying the events that led up to the major world wars or other significant historical events would allow society to chart a different and more favorable course in the future.

Just as difficult as convincing students to realize the importance of studying history is the search for useful and interesting supplementary materials that present historical events in a context that can be easily understood. The volumes in Lucent Books' World History Series attempt to present a broad, balanced, and penetrating view of the march of history. Ancient Egypt's important wars and rulers, for example, are presented against the rich and colorful backdrop of Egyptian religious, social, and cultural developments. The series engages the reader by enhancing historical events with these cultural contexts. For example, in *Ancient Greece*, the text covers the role of women in that society. Slavery is discussed in *The Roman Empire*, as well as how slaves earned their freedom. The numerous and varied aspects of everyday life in these and other societies are explored in each volume of the series. Additionally, the series covers the major political, cultural, and philosophical ideas as the torch of civilization is passed from ancient Mesopotamia and Egypt, through Greece, Rome, medieval Europe, and other world cultures, to the modern day.

The material in the series is formatted in a thorough, precise, and organized manner. Each volume offers the reader a comprehensive and clearly written overview of an important historical event or period. The topic under discussion is placed in a broad, historical context. For example, *The Italian Renaissance* begins with a discussion of the High Middle Ages and the loss of central control that allowed certain Italian cities to develop artistically. The book ends by looking forward to the Reformation and interpreting the societal changes that grew out of the Renaissance. Thus, students are not only involved in an historical era, but also enveloped by the events leading up to that era and the events following it.

One important and unique feature in the World History Series is the primary and secondary source quotations that richly supplement each volume. These quotes are useful in a number of ways. First, they allow students access to sources they would not normally be exposed to because of the difficulty and obscurity of the original source. The quotations range from interesting anecdotes to farsighted cultural perspectives and are drawn from historical witnesses both past and present. Second, the quotes demonstrate how and where historians themselves derive their information on the past as they strive to reach a consensus on historical events. Lastly, all of the quotes are footnoted, familiarizing students with the citation process and allowing them to verify quotes and/or look up the original source if the quote piques their interest.

Finally, the books in the World History Series provide a detailed launching point for further research. Each book contains a bibliography specifically geared toward student research. A second, annotated bibliography introduces students to all the sources the author consulted when compiling the book. A chronology of important dates gives students an overview, at a glance, of the topic covered. Where applicable, a glossary of terms is included.

In short, the series is designed not only to acquaint readers with the basics of history, but also to make them aware that their lives are a part of an ongoing human saga. Perhaps they will then come to the same realization as famed historian Arnold Toynbee. In his monumental work, *A Study of History,* he wrote about becoming aware of history flowing through him in a mighty current, and of his own life "welling like a wave in the flow of this vast tide."

IMPORTANT DATES IN THE HISTORY OF THE LOUISIANA PURCHASE

1762–1763
France gives up western Louisiana, plus New Orleans, to Spain and eastern Louisiana to England.

1783
England transfers eastern Louisiana to the United States.

1682
René-Robert Cavelier de La Salle leads a party down the length of the Mississippi to the Gulf of Mexico and claims the river and its eastern and western basins for France; he names this territory Louisiana.

1784
The Spanish close the lower Mississippi River and New Orleans to foreign trade.

1675	1700	1725	1760	1780	1800

1795
The Treaty of San Lorenzo allows Americans to navigate the lower Mississippi River and to deposit goods duty-free in New Orleans.

1722
New Orleans becomes the capital of Louisiana.

1699
Pierre Le Moyne, sieur d'Iberville, establishes France's first settlement in Louisiana.

1800
France and Spain draw up the Treaty of San Ildefonso on October 1, agreeing to the return of western Louisiana and New Orleans to France.

1801
Robert R. Livingston arrives in France to begin negotiations for New Orleans and western Florida with France's minister of foreign affairs.

1802

October 15: Spain signs the Treaty of San Ildefonso, officially giving France title to Louisiana;

1803

April 11: France offers to sell Louisiana to the United States; April 12: James Monroe arrives in Paris to aid in negotiations with the French; May 2: The treaty for the Louisiana Purchase is signed; May 22: Napoléon ratifies the Louisiana Purchase Treaty; October 20: The U.S. Senate ratifies the Louisiana Purchase Treaty; November 30: France takes possession of the Louisiana Territory; December 20: France hands lower Louisiana over to the United States.

1804

March 9: The United States takes possession of upper Louisiana; March 26: The United States splits Louisiana into the Orleans Territory and the Louisiana District; May 14: Meriwether Lewis and William Clark start up the Missouri River.

1812
The Orleans Territory is admitted to the Union as the state of Louisiana; the United States and England go to war.

1819
The United States and Spain fix the southwestern and western boundaries of the Louisiana Purchase region, and Spain sells Florida to America.

800	1805	1810	1815	1820	1905

1806
The Grand Excursion explores the Red River; Zebulon Pike reaches the Rocky Mountains; Lewis and Clark return to St. Louis.

1815
American forces, commanded by Andrew Jackson, repel a British attack on New Orleans.

1907
Oklahoma, the last of the Louisiana Purchase, becomes a state.

1818
Jackson seizes the remainder of Florida; the United States and Great Britain agree on the northern border of the Missouri Territory.

1810
Part of western Florida is added to the Orleans Territory.

1821
Missouri is admitted as a state.

The New Territory

The 1803 Louisiana Purchase was the biggest real estate deal in American history and one of the largest in world history. For $15 million (about 3¢ an acre), the United States bought from France a huge 830,000-square-mile triangle of land in the heart of North America. The impact of the purchase on the United States was immediate and long lasting.

THE GOVERNMENT AND LAND DEALS

One of the important consequences of the Louisiana Purchase was to establish the federal government's right to acquire and add territory to the United States, an action not mentioned in the U.S. Constitution. This right to obtain new lands would help strengthen the authority and power of the central government, which would have the sole responsibility of administering Louisiana and other new territories until their sections achieved statehood.

Within fifteen years of the Louisiana Purchase, the U.S. government would exercise this new authority when it bought Florida from Spain. Later purchases would include Texas, the Southwest, and

California, all bought in 1848 from Mexico after that country's defeat by the United States in the Mexican War. In 1853 the Gadsden Purchase would give America another chunk of northern Mexico, and in 1867 the United States would buy Alaska from Russia. The ultimate outcome of all of these purchases would be to extend the United States from the Atlantic Ocean to the Pacific and see that the country took over the entire center of North America.

THE UNITED STATES DOUBLES

The immediate result of the Louisiana Purchase was more modest but still dramatic, as it almost doubled the size of the United States. At the time of the purchase, the nation covered 1 million square miles and stretched from the Atlantic Ocean to the Mississippi River. Its northern border, as it remains today, was Canada. Its southern border was Florida, which belonged to Spain. This Spanish possession consisted of the current state plus a strip of land running along the Gulf of Mexico and ending at the Mississippi River.

The territory of Louisiana, named in the seventeenth century for the French king

The Louisiana Territory was named in honor of King Louis XIV of France.

Louis XIV, was almost as large as the entire United States, covering almost 830,000 square miles. It was thus immense, being larger than the combined areas of Italy, Spain, Portugal, France, Switzerland, Germany, Belgium, the Netherlands, and the British Isles. Out of the region would be carved, in part or whole, thirteen states: Arkansas, Colorado, Iowa, Kansas, Louisiana, Minnesota, Missouri, Montana, Nebraska, North Dakota, Oklahoma, South Dakota, and Wyoming.

A Land Unknown

Louisiana would make the United States a wealthy nation, for it would prove rich in gold, silver, and other valuable ores as well as vast timber reserves and rich grazing and farmlands. Possession of this region would eventually make U.S. mining and agriculture among the most productive in the world.

However, in 1803 only rumors of these riches circulated among the settlers in the region. The Louisiana Territory was mostly blank on the maps of the world.

Even the number of people living in the territory was in doubt since no census existed. The French believed that the population was at least sixty thousand but less than one hundred thousand. Of these inhabitants, half were thought to be Europeans and Americans; the other half were black slaves and Native Americans. Only the Native Americans were scattered throughout the territory. The whites and blacks were concentrated mainly in settlements along the Mississippi River, with the largest population being in New Orleans.

Blurry Borders

If knowledge of Louisiana's resources and population were poor, so was information about its boundaries. In theory, Louisiana was the western basin, or watershed, of the Mississippi River. In other words, it contained all of the western streams and rivers that fed water into North America's great central river. Most of the Mississippi's eastern basin was already part of the United States.

In actuality, some of the western drainage area proved to be within territory belonging to Great Britain in the north and Spain in the west and southwest. This misunderstanding about what was and was not a part of Louisiana arose because the region's exact borders were unknown. For instance, the western boundary of Louisiana was the Continental Divide, which runs along the crest of the Rocky Mountains and separates rivers and streams flowing westward from those moving eastward. However, in 1803 the exact location of the divide was unknown.

Louisiana's borders with Canada and the Spanish southwest were equally unclear. Only its eastern margin, formed by the Mississippi River, was relatively clearcut. Yet, even here, there was confusion about Louisiana's southeastern border with Florida. Historian Alexander DeConde observes,

> As the French had explained during the treaty negotiations, the boundaries of the Louisiana territory that the United States had acquired were vague. The American government knew only that its new uncharted empire ran south from Canada's Lake of the Woods to New Orleans and west from the Mississippi River to the Rocky Mountains.[1]

RIVERS AND PLAINS

What was not in doubt was that the United States now controlled the Mississippi River.

A large portion of the Louisiana Purchase encompassed the area known today as the Great Plains.

Except for a small portion of the river's southeastern bank, which was part of Spanish Florida, the entire Mississippi, from its northern reaches to its mouth on the Gulf of Mexico, belonged to the United States. At the time of purchase, this twenty-three-hundred-mile river was already an important waterway for American trade, and U.S. possession of the river guaranteed that this flow of goods would not only continue but that it would also grow until Mississippi River traffic became crucial to the U.S. economy. As then-president Thomas Jefferson wrote, "The acquisition of New Orleans would of itself have been a great thing, but that of Louisiana is inappreciable [invaluable], because . . . [it gives] us sole dominion of the Mississippi."[2]

But the United States gained much more than just control of the Mississippi River. As the scholar Marshall Sprague notes, the "infant United States acquired the largest and most valuable river system on earth,"[3] for many other rivers were also now added to the United States. Crossing the Louisiana Territory from west to east to empty into the Mississippi were the Missouri, the Arkansas, and the Red Rivers. Several other major Louisiana Territory rivers, such as the Kansas, the Platte, and the Yellowstone, fed the Missouri, a river as long as the Mississippi.

Except for the Mississippi, these Louisiana rivers flowed in large part through the Great Plains, a high, dry, grass-covered plateau rising west of the Mississippi and stretching to the Rocky Mountains. Given to frigid winters and blazing summers, this region was home to giant herds of buffalo and pronghorn an-

Decades before the Louisiana Purchase, Americans had already begun the settlement of frontier areas.

telope. The rivers would provide roads through, and later into, the Great Plains for people and material as well as sites for towns and cities.

LOOKING WEST

Even before the Louisiana Purchase, the United States was facing west. In the quarter century before the purchase, tens of thousands of settlers had poured over the Appalachian Mountains into Ohio, Kentucky, and Tennessee, all the way to the Mississippi. But this western movement did not stop there; although Louisiana was not yet U.S. territory at the time, many Americans crossed into that land, sometimes as trappers, sometimes as farmers.

The buying of Louisiana made certain that westward migration would remain an important part of the American story. As Sprague writes, "Possession of the empire [the Louisiana Territory] . . . set [the United States and] its people permanently on a course that would lead them in no time at all to the Pacific Ocean."[4]

A flood of American explorers and settlers entered the Louisiana Territory almost immediately after the U.S. takeover. But the story of the exploration and settlement of Louisiana was already old by the time these Americans made their way into their new possession.

1 The Making of Louisiana

With the Louisiana Purchase, the United States became the third nation to possess this vast North American territory. In the past both France and Spain had claimed the land. In the sixteen century, the Spanish were the first whites to explore the region, and the French were its first white settlers a century and a half later.

However, these Europeans were not the first people to explore and settle the land that would become Louisiana. No one ac-

tually knows who first discovered the Mississippi River or who first entered the western lands drained by it, but they were certainly Native Americans. The first evidence of humans living along the Mississippi and in its western basin dates back to at least 200 B.C. By the time the first Europeans ventured into these regions, Indians had long-established settlements on the Mississippi and the other rivers of the Mississippi basin.

Indian cultures flourished along the banks of the Mississippi River hundreds of years before Europeans explored the region.

THE SUN CULT

In his Travels in the Interior of North America, 1751–1762, *the French naval officer Jean-Bernard Bossu describes the sun cult found among the Natchez Indians, who lived along the lower Mississippi River.*

"The Natchez . . . had several villages ruled by individual chiefs, who in turn were governed by the great chief of the entire nation. All of these chiefs were called 'Suns,' and . . . the Great Sun, their sovereign, . . . wore on his chest a picture of the sun from which he claimed descent. . . .

The ceremonies of this sun cult were rather august [lofty]. The high priest arose before sunrise and walked solemnly at the head of his people. He carried a calumet [ceremonial pipe], and, in order to honor the sun, blew the first puff of smoke in its direction. Staring at the sun's first rays and extending his arms toward the sky, each worshipper howled in turn after the high priest. Then they all prostrated themselves [threw themselves down]. The women brought their children to this ceremony and made them assume the positions required by the rite. . . .

They [the Natchez] had a temple in which burned an eternal flame. The priests . . . were permitted to use the wood of only one type of tree. If . . . the flame went out, the horrified nation put the responsible priests to death. . . .

When the sovereign died, his wives and several of his subjects were put to death so that they could accompany him to the grave. The lesser Suns carefully followed the same custom. According to the law, when a female relative of the Suns died, her husband was put to death too."

THE MISSISSIPPIANS

When those first European explorers reached the Mississippi River, they encountered the people of the Mississippian culture, who lived along the middle and lower reaches of the river as well as over most of what would later become the southern United States. Mississippian culture dated back to at least A.D. 800 and was the successor to an earlier society, the Hopewell, which had died out several centuries before.

Mississippian life revolved around large towns or small cities. As Michael Coe, Dean Snow, and Elizabeth Benson explain,

> [Their] settlements . . . qualified as true towns, sometimes as preindustrial cities. . . . Mississippian towns typically contain from 1 to 20 flat-topped mounds that served as platforms for temples or other public structures. In some cases these structures were residences for the elite. The sites were often

stockaded [surrounded by a wooden wall], with residences both inside and outside the stockade lines.[5]

Ruled by a hereditary king and his family, a typical Mississippian town had a central plaza, at one end of which was the royal palace. Placed atop a mound, generally from ten to twelve feet high, this residence was trimmed with shells and painted in bright colors. Ordinary citizens lived in adobe houses, which were whitewashed with a mixture of white clay and chalk. Other buildings included cooking houses and saunas.

The largest of the Mississippian cities was Cahokia, near present-day East St. Louis, Illinois. At its height, around the middle of the twelfth century, Cahokia's population was ten thousand, and it had over one hundred mounds, making it the largest urban area north of Mexico.

FARMERS AND WARRIORS

The Mississippians were farmers who raised corn, beans, and squash. The harvested crops were stored in small wooden huts, which were raised up above the ground on posts and surrounded the palace. Hunting and fishing supplied additional food. Inside some Mississippian cities were ponds stocked with fish.

These people farmed only the land along rivers, which could be worked easily with digging sticks and hoes used for planting. The Mississippians lacked plows with which to work harder ground. As town and city populations expanded, fierce rivalries broke out among neighboring communities over croplands, and these rivalries often led to wars.

PLAINS DWELLERS

Other groups of Native Americans also lived in the region that would become the Louisiana Territory. Along the fringe of the Great Plains, nomadic bands of hunters lived off of the buffalo, just as they had for almost two thousand years. These nomads traveled and hunted on foot. The horse had become extinct some ten thousand years ago in the Americas, and until the arrival of Europeans, North American Indians had no other beasts of burden except the dog, which the plains nomads used to pull a small vehicle called a travois, a small platform lashed to two sticks.

Few people actually lived on the Great Plains themselves, and those few dwelled in farming communities, which had begun springing up around A.D. 800. Like the Mississippians, these people farmed along rivers, growing corn and beans. Many of them also spent part of the year hunting buffalo. The plains dwellers lived in circular stockades, or fortified villages, surrounded by dry moats. Inside were living quarters, called lodges, and several families shared a single lodge. Each village also had a number of underground food storage pits.

THE FIRST EUROPEANS

In 1519 the Spanish sea captain Alonso Alvárez de Piñeda and his crew became the first Europeans to sight the future Louisiana Territory when they sailed along its

In 1541 a group of Spaniards led by Hernando de Soto (center) became the first Europeans to cross the Mississippi River.

southern coast. They may also have spotted the mouth of the Mississippi River, for they certainly passed it. But Piñeda made no record of such a sighting. He noted only a few of the river mouths he discovered, having little interest in the region. His mission was rather to discover the Strait of Anian, a supposed passage between the Gulf of Mexico and the Pacific Ocean that would give Spanish mariners a quick route to China. Eventually, Europeans would realize that no such waterway existed.

The first Spanish explorers to set foot in Louisiana were members of a party led by Hernando de Soto. This expedition had two goals. First, the Spaniards were anxious to find cultures rich in gold and other treasures, as had been the Aztec and the Inca civilizations. Soto himself had taken part in the conquest and plunder of the latter. Second, the Spanish hoped to find the Strait of Anian, for which Piñeda had been searching a quarter century earlier.

On May 18, 1539, Soto sailed from Cuba with 620 men, landing in Florida. Although the expedition actually landed in the present-day state of Florida, the Spanish called most of the continent north of Mexico Florida and mistakenly believed it to be just slightly larger than Mexico.

SOTO CROSSES THE MISSISSIPPI

Over the next two years, the Spaniards moved north and then west. From the beginning, they waged war on the Native

Americans they met, including the Mississippians. As Sprague notes, Soto chased "gold rumors all over the Deep South, murdering hordes of . . . [Native Americans] and losing hundreds of his own soldiers in skirmishes and from disease."[6] Those Indians not killed were often enslaved and then worked to death.

On May 8, 1541, at a site some seventy-five miles south of where Memphis, Tennessee, would one day stand, Soto and his men became the first Europeans to stand on the banks of the Mississippi River, which they called the Great River of Florida. Then they became the first Europeans to cross the river and stand in what would become the Louisiana Territory. Tramping through much of present-day Arkansas, Soto searched frantically and fruitlessly for the Strait of Anian and gold.

SHIPBUILDING ON THE MISSISSIPPI

After Hernando de Soto died, his surviving men, under the command of Luis de Moscoso, eventually sailed down the Mississippi to safety. In a memoir, excerpted in Exploring the Great River, *an anonymous Portuguese member of the expedition later described the building of the vessels for this journey.*

"The Governor [Moscoso] ordered them to gather all the chains which everyone had to keep Indians in, all the iron anyone had. . . . He set up a forge to make nails and had timber cut. A Portuguese . . . had learned to saw timber with a long saw. . . . He taught others, who helped him saw timber. A Man for Genoa [Italy], who it pleased God to keep alive, for without him we never could have come out of the [Mississippi] country, was a shipmaker. He, with four or five . . . carpenters who cut his planks . . . , made the brigantines [small sailing crafts]. . . .

The Indians, seeing the brigantines . . . , feared the ships would be used against them. When the Governor asked them for mantles [cloaks] to make sails with, they thought it wise to be friendly and came many times, bringing many mantles and great store[s] of fish. . . . The Indians also brought cords, and they [the Spanish] made cables [rope] out of the bark of mulberry trees. They [the Spanish] made stirrups of wood [for their horses] and used their iron stirrups for making anchors. . . .

When the time came to embark, they [the Spanish] put their corn into the brigantines, and in large canoes tied together in twos. They put twenty-two of their best horses into the ships. . . . They left . . . the second day of July, 1543."

He also continued his campaign of terror against Native Americans.

After a year, Soto found himself back at the Mississippi. His expedition was short on supplies, particularly ammunition, and Soto realized that he had to admit failure and find a way to Spanish-controlled Mexico. Before he could make any plans, Soto died suddenly of a fever on May 21, 1542.

After Soto's death, the survivors of the expedition once more turned west, marching through future Louisiana in an attempt to reach Mexico City. However, after a thousand-mile trek, they turned back when they reached the drylands of central Texas and realized that they could not find enough food or water to keep going. The following year, 1543, they sailed down the Mississippi in crude vessels and then along the gulf coast to Spanish Mexico. Dressed in rags, the 311 survivors, half the number that had set out from Cuba, had nothing to show for their four years of hardship except memories of what they considered a wild, savage land.

Golden Cities

In June 1541, at roughly the same time as Soto was crossing the Arkansas River near the future site of Little Rock, another Spanish explorer, Francisco Vásquez de Coronado, and a small band of followers were wading the same river in what would become the western part of the Louisiana Territory and then Kansas. The two expeditions would eventually approach within 370 miles of each other.

Like Soto, Coronado was searching for gold. In February 1540 he left Mexico City with some three hundred Spanish soldiers and marched north into current-day New Mexico. The Spaniards' goal was the rumored seven golden cities of Cibola, but instead, they found the pueblos of the Zuni Indians, which were quickly overrun and captured by Coronado. These Native Americans were farmers and hunters and had no more gold than did the Indians Soto was persecuting farther east. Coronado's march was not marked by bloodbaths as was Soto's, but his command killed Native Americans who resisted the Spanish invaders or refused to give up their religious beliefs for Christianity.

The Kingdoms of Kansas

Although disappointed in the reality of Cibola, Coronado was not finished. He and thirty horsemen, known as the Chosen Thirty, were soon headed northeast into the western reaches of the future Louisiana Territory. A Zuni slave had told the Spanish leader of two wealthy kingdoms, Thegayo and Quivira, whose location was in present-day Kansas. During their journey east, Coronado and the Chosen Thirty became the first Europeans to find the Continental Divide, which would later mark the western border of the Louisiana Territory, and to enter Colorado and Kansas. They marveled at the great herds of buffalo and the sprawled prairie dog towns of the Great Plains.

However, Coronado again failed to find treasure. Like the seven golden cities,

Francisco Vásquez de Coronado explored present-day Kansas in search of wealthy Native American Kingdoms.

Thegayo and Quivira turned out to be more myth than reality. In Kansas, all that the Spanish found were poor Plains farming villages. Discouraged, Coronado turned around and rejoined the rest of his command, which then returned to Mexico City in 1542.

The End of the Mississippians

After the failures of the Soto and Coronado expeditions, the Spanish abandoned the Mississippi and the lands it drained. And, even though they still claimed this territory, they made no further effort to explore, settle, or exploit it. And, for 130 years, no record exists of a European visiting the region.

During this time, the Mississippian culture came to a sudden end. Its towns and cities were abandoned, and the Mississippians disappeared. A few people, the Natchez and the Creek, still farmed and built temple mounds as had the Mississippians. However, their communities were only small villages with one or two small mounds, nothing on the order of the Mississippian city of Cahokia.

What caused the sudden disappearance of the Mississippians remains a mystery. Soto biographer David Ewing Duncan speculates that Soto's treatment of Native Americans was responsible:

> The collapse of their [the Mississippian] civilization . . . [was] caused in part by Soto's systematic looting of their villages, towns, and cities; the kidnapping . . . and murder of Mississippian leaders; and the deaths of tens of thousands killed in warfare, from being worked to death as slaves and porters, from starvation when Soto's army plundered food supplies, and from contracting Old World diseases [such as smallpox] to which they had no immunity.[7]

Disease may have been helped by the poor sanitation in Mississippian towns, which had no sewer systems and thus no way to dispose of human waste.

THE FRENCH PUSH SOUTH

On June 17, 1673, two birch-bark canoes with seven men sailed out of the Wisconsin River and into the Mississippi. The seven were French explorers who had been sent out by the governor of New France (later Canada) to find a water route to the Pacific. The expedition's leaders were Louis Jolliet and Jacques Marquette. Jolliet had been born in New France and was a successful trader and map maker, and Marquette was a French Jesuit, a member of the Society of Jesus. The Jesuits were Catholic missionaries, and Marquette's missionary activities had made him an expert on the customs of Native Americans. The other five men were voyageurs, who ferried French fur trappers to distant regions and then returned them and their furs back to New France.

Turning south, the French expedition coasted along a stretch of the Mississippi that would one day mark the border between the states of Wisconsin and Iowa. Over the next two months, the explorers traveled one thousand miles down the Mississippi. It was a trip that led them past the mouths of other rivers, most notably the turbulent Missouri and the more serene Ohio. The Missouri particularly impressed Marquette, who wrote, "I have seen . . . nothing more dreadful. An accumulation [collection] of large and entire trees, branches and floating islands, was issuing from the mouth of the river . . . with such intensity that we could not without great danger risk passing through it."[8]

By the time the explorers reached the mouth of the Missouri, they had given up

Frenchmen Louis Jolliet and Jacques Marquette explored one thousand miles of the Mississippi River in search of a water route to the Pacific Ocean.

THE "WILD CATTLE" OF LOUISIANA

In the following account by Jacques Marquette, reprinted in Exploring the Great River, *the French explorer describes his party's first encounter in 1673 with the American buffalo, which Marquette calls "wild cattle."*

"When we reached the latitude of forty-one degrees . . . we found that . . . wild cattle replaced the other animals. . . . They are not any longer than cattle, but they are nearly as large again and much heavier. When our party killed one, it took three men to move it. . . . The head is very large. The forehead is flat. Its horns are a foot and a half apart, being exactly like the horns of our cattle except that they are black and much larger. Under the neck, they have a large fold of skin hanging down and there is a high hump on their back. . . .

Moreover, these wild cattle are fierce. . . . When attacked, a buffalo will try to catch a man on its horns and toss him in the air, then the beast will throw him to the ground and trample him underfoot, killing him. When a hunter fires at a buffalo from a distance with either bow and arrow or a gun, he must, immediately after the shot, throw himself down and hide in the grass. If the buffalo sees who fired, it will run at him and attack him. Since the beast's legs are thick and rather short, it does not usually run very fast, but when angry it can move quickly."

Jacques Marquette came across herds of buffalo, which he called "wild cattle," during his exploration of the Mississippi River.

the idea that the Mississippi would lead to the Pacific, for it was obviously flowing south. After talking with local Indians, Marquette became convinced that the Missouri was the pathway to the Pacific. The Indians told him that the river came from mountains in the West and that on the other side of the mountains was another river that flowed into the sea. Marquette believed that the western ocean was only a one- or two-week journey away because, like the Spanish before him, he thought that North America was much narrower than it really was.

The explorers pushed on until they reached the mouth of the Arkansas River. The Native Americans of the region told them that the Mississippi emptied into the Gulf of Mexico. Jolliet, Marquette, and the others decided to return home. They believed that they had important information to report and were afraid that, if they did follow the river to the Gulf, they would be captured and imprisoned by the Spanish.

La Salle's Grand Scheme

A report of Jolliet and Marquette's discoveries soon reached a French adventurer, René-Robert Cavelier de La Salle. La Salle had arrived in New France in 1666, seeking and finding his fortune as a landholder and fur trader. He had spent some time exploring south of the Great Lakes in what would become Ohio.

La Salle realized that the great river Jolliet and Marquette had sailed along was the same one discovered by Soto. More importantly, he became convinced that France had to set up forts and settlements running from New France to the Mississippi and then along the river to the Gulf of Mexico. In doing so, France would be able to dominate the interior of North America and could freeze out its colonial rivals, Spain and England, the latter of whom now had thriving colonies on the Atlantic coast of the continent.

La Salle made two visits to France, and in 1677 he finally wrangled a royal charter from King Louis XIV allowing him to explore the Mississippi and then to build as many forts as he wanted. The charter also gave La Salle a monopoly on the trade in buffalo hides. What King Louis did not give was money. La Salle had to use his own wealth, as well as borrow heavily from various merchants in New France, to finance his scheme.

Down the Mississippi

La Salle gave up his idea of a line of forts when, in December 1680, the first two he built on the Illinois River were destroyed by the Iroquois, with whom the French had been at war since the founding of New France earlier in the seventeenth century. La Salle turned his efforts completely to exploration of the Mississippi, which he finally reached in February 1682.

La Salle's party numbered fifty-four, being a mix of French and Native Americans. His fleet of canoes soon passed the raging mouth of the Missouri, which impressed the explorers with the mudlike quality of its water, there being so much soil dissolved in the river. Much later, this characteristic of Missouri water would earn this river the name Big Muddy.

THE LAND BECOMES LOUISIANA

After a month's travel, the La Salle party passed the mouth of the Arkansas River, the southernmost point reached by Jolliet and Marquette a decade earlier. Then, in early April, the Mississippi water turned brackish and finally salty. They were close to the meeting of river and sea. Then the river split into three channels. On April 9, after exploring all three channels, La Salle and his followers stood and looked out over the blue gulf waters. They had reached the mouth of the Mississippi.

La Salle erected a pole and a cross painted with France's coat of arms. He then claimed all of the land, east and west, drained by the Mississippi in the name of King Louis XIV. La Salle also named the new French territory Louisiana after Louis. In taking possession of Louisiana for France, La Salle ignored the prior Spanish claim and any rights of ownership by Native Americans, whose ancestors had been living on the land for untold generations.

René-Robert Cavelier de La Salle claimed all the lands east and west drained by the Mississippi River for France, naming the area Louisiana.

La Salle wanted to be able to find the Mississippi from the sea, so he measured the latitude of the river's mouth. Since the seventeenth century had no way of determining longitude, he could not pinpoint his location. Unfortunately for La Salle, his measurement of latitude did not help him when, three years later, he led a French naval expedition into the Gulf of Mexico searching for the Mississippi. The French ships ended up at the right latitude but five hundred miles too far west on the coast of Texas. Repeated attempts to find the river on foot failed, and on March 19, 1687, part of La Salle's discontented crew mutinied and killed him.

COLONIZING LOUISIANA

Back in France, interest in Louisiana was almost nonexistent. Louis XIV was con-

LA SALLE CLAIMS LOUISIANA

Reproduced in The Journeys of Réné Robert Cavelier, Sieur de la Salle, *is the following proclamation read by the French explorer La Salle when he claimed Louisiana for France.*

"In the name of the most high, mighty, invincible and victorious Prince, Louis the Great, by the Grace of God, King of France . . . , Fourteenth of that name, this ninth day of April, one thousand six hundred and eighty-two, I [La Salle], in virtue of the commission of his Majesty which I hold in my hand, and which may be seen by all whom it may concern, have taken, and now do take, in the name of his Majesty and of his successors to the crown, possession of this country of Louisiana, the seas, harbors, ports, bays, adjacent straits, and all the nations, people, provinces, cities, towns, villages, mines, minerals, fisheries, streams and rivers comprised in the extent of said Louisiana, from . . . its [the Mississippi's] source . . . as far as its mouth at the sea, or Gulf of Mexico . . . ; upon the assurance which we have received from all . . . [the] nations [of Native Americans] that we are the first Europeans who have descended or ascended the . . . River Colbert [Mississippi]; hereby protesting against all those who may in future undertake to invade any or all of these countries, people, or lands . . . to the prejudice [injury] of the right of his Majesty. . . . Of which . . . I hereby take to witness those who hear me, . . . as required by law."

John Law's efforts to build up France's settlements in Louisiana ended in economic disaster.

sumed with European affairs and the maintenance of a large army, with which he pursued a series of wars to promote French interests in Europe. He had no time and almost no money to spare for the undeveloped land named after him. Thus, no permanent colony was organized until over a decade after La Salle's death.

Finally, in April 1699, under the direction of a young naval officer, Pierre Le Moyne, sieur d'Iberville, a small colony of forty-five people was planted in Louisiana. The colony's purpose was to make clear—particularly to England—that the territory belonged to France. England was very interested in gaining possession of the Mississippi. Like La Salle, they saw it as the key to domination of the continental interior. The English had sent one ship up the Mississippi to establish trade relations with the Indians there. And, from the east, other English traders were pushing over the Appalachians into Louisiana.

As with La Salle, Louis XIV refused to provide adequate funds for the new colony, despite Le Moyne's constant reminders that, short of war, the settling of Louisiana was the only way to keep the English at bay. Thus, the Louisiana colony grew slowly and fared poorly, often half forgotten by France. It relocated itself a number of times over the next fifteen years, looking for a hospitable home.

THE COMPANY OF THE WEST

Not until 1716 did the fortunes of the Louisiana colony improve. Louis XIV had died the previous year, and a Scottish economist, John Law, was able to persuade the French government to give him a private charter to develop Louisiana, at least along the lower reaches of the Mississippi. Law quickly formed the Company of the West and was able to coax many people in France to invest in the venture. A shrewd promoter, he painted an overly optimistic picture of quick money from mining and farming, despite the fact that no mines were operating in Louisiana and little farming was being done.

As DeConde notes, Law pumped up the population of the colony by rounding up and sending "vagrants, prostitutes, criminals, and other social outcasts. The colony became a dumping ground for political exiles."[9] Law also imported several thousand black slaves. Within four years, the colony grew from less than five hundred settlers to over eight thousand, not counting the slaves.

Few of the people Law imported to Louisiana were cut out to be pioneers and face the hardships of living with the swamps and heat of the southern Mississippi. Farming was not easy in this area, and colonists were soon dying of starvation and disease.

Additionally, the enterprise was costing a lot of money but producing no profits. When stories of the hardship and the lack of profits reached France, investors began pulling their money out. Few got more than a small percentage of their investments back since the Company of the West was heavily in debt. Speculation in the company had been so widespread that its collapse actually damaged the French economy. Law, who had become the minister of finance, had to flee the country. This economic disaster became known as the Mississippi Bubble because, like a soap bubble, the scheme expanded until it exploded, leaving nothing.

NEW ORLEANS

Although the Company of the West failed, it did improve the Louisiana colony. Lumbering and the farming of corn, rice, and tobacco were established. Unfortunately, few French merchants found it profitable to ship these goods from Louisiana.

Perhaps the company's most important legacy was the port of New Orleans. Founded in 1718, New Orleans was the brainchild of the governor general of

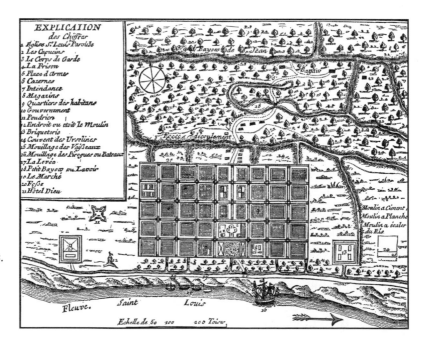

An early map of New Orleans. Founded in 1718, New Orleans grew rapidly and became the capital of the Louisiana Territory in 1722.

Louisiana, Jean-Baptiste Le Moyne, sieur de Bienville, younger brother of Pierre Le Moyne. The settlement's site, some one hundred miles north of the Gulf of Mexico on the Mississippi's east bank, allowed it to control traffic on the river and from the sea. Thus, goods could be easily transferred from river craft to oceangoing ships and vice versa.

Construction of the port took several years and was hampered by sullen convict laborers, heat, mosquitoes, and two hurricanes. The city's first residents were a mix of company officials, soldiers, voyageurs and trappers from New France, Native Americans, slaves, convicts, and prostitutes. In 1722 New Orleans became the capital of Louisiana.

FORGOTTEN LOUISIANA

After the failure of the Company of the West, France's enthusiasm for Louisiana dwindled. Neither the colony nor its new port city of New Orleans were profitable, and no one in France had any desire to make them so. Immigration to Louisiana dropped to a trickle, and by the middle of the eighteenth century, the colony's European population only numbered around two thousand. Nor were those who came interested in settling down. The historian James K. Hosmer remarks, "When immigrants appear, it is to hunt gold or fur-bearing beasts . . . , in desultory [random] wandering, rather than to till the soil and establish homes."[10]

The colony remained centered on the lower Mississippi, with no settlements north of the Arkansas River. Exploration of western Louisiana did continue, for the French were still determined to find a waterway through North America to the Pacific. For the next quarter century, explorers followed the Missouri and its tributaries west and north, and although these adventurers did not achieve the Pacific, two of them, Pierre and Louis-Joseph La Vérendrye, reached the Rocky Mountains in early 1743. There, they buried a plate with the French coat of arms, marking the western border of Louisiana.

There was little attention paid to the La Vérendryes' accomplishment either in southern Louisiana or in France. The expedition had not brought back a shortcut to the Pacific nor any other source of quick wealth. In any case, official interest was now focused east rather than west.

THE FRENCH AND INDIAN WAR

Although the French government had little affection or use for Louisiana, it resented the increasing English presence in the eastern part of the colony. The English traders had been followed by settlers who made their way into the Ohio country by crossing the Allegheny Mountains. The French attempted to counter this British invasion by building a series of forts in eastern Louisiana and by allying themselves with various Native American tribes, whom they encouraged to attack the English. In 1754 French-English friction sparked the French and Indian War (known as the Seven Years' War in Europe).

Initially the French did well, but in the end they lost the war. This defeat resulted in a French retreat from North America. In November 1762 France agreed to transfer western Louisiana and New Orleans to Spain. The Spanish had entered the war late as France's ally but had managed to lose Florida to the British. Thus, the French offered half of Louisiana as compensation for that loss.

Three months later, in February 1763, the Treaty of Paris ended the war and gave England both New France, or Canada, and Louisiana east of the Mississippi, except for New Orleans. Although Canada had been conquered by the British, eastern Louisiana was exchanged willingly by the French in return for several Caribbean islands, valuable for their sugar production, which had been captured by the British during the war.

SPAIN TAKES COMMAND

It was not until 1771 that the French flag came down over western Louisiana and the Spanish took possession. Ironically, it was during this period, when the French

After suffering defeat in the French and Indian War, France lost control of all of its North American colonies.

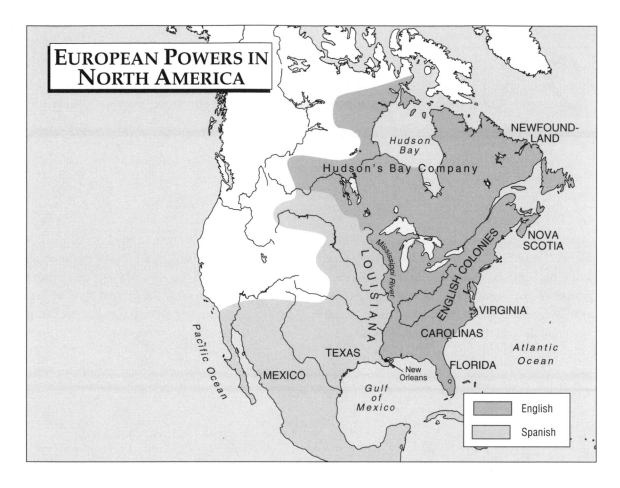

EUROPEAN POWERS IN NORTH AMERICA

NEWFOUND-LAND

Hudson Bay

Hudson's Bay Company

NOVA SCOTIA

Mississippi River

LOUISIANA

ENGLISH COLONIES

VIRGINIA

CAROLINAS

Atlantic Ocean

TEXAS

FLORIDA

MEXICO

New Orleans

Gulf of Mexico

Pacific Ocean

English

Spanish

were preparing to abandon their colony, that Louisiana's French inhabitants finally started settling the region's northern reaches. Historian James Q. Howard writes,

> [The] Village du Côte, now St. Charles, on the Missouri River, was the first village built . . . north of the Arkansas [River]. The date of this settlement was 1762. On the 15th of February, 1764, St. Louis was founded. . . . St. Louis [would become] the future capital of upper Louisiana.[11]

With the final departure of the French, it was the Spanish, not the English, who now controlled the Mississippi River. As the scholar E. Wilson Lyon points out, "The strategic location of . . . New Orleans, together with the land west of the Mississippi [and the city], would give Spain complete control of navigation of that great artery of commerce."[12] Exercise of that control would prove increasingly more difficult as English, and then within a few years American, settlers pushed into the former eastern Louisiana and began looking on the Mississippi as their river.

2 Uneasy Relations

In 1783 the Revolutionary War concluded with the signing of the second Treaty of Paris. The former thirteen British colonies were recognized as the independent United States of America. Included in the new nation's territory was what had once been the eastern half of Louisiana. Florida, which the United States would have liked as well, was returned to Spain.

From its beginning as a nation, America had its eye on Louisiana. Many Americans, particularly those west of the Appalachians, saw Louisiana as a land being held in trust for them by Spain. And they

George Washington takes command of the Continental Army. After winning its independence from Great Britain, the United States looked to acquire more territory in the west.

Outposts established along the eastern shores of the Mississippi River allowed the United States to protect its interests in that region.

were convinced that, one day in the not-too-distant future, they would make that land a part of the United States. Americans would do all in their power to see that Louisiana's next owner would be America, not another European nation.

DESTINY AND TRADE

The possessive attitude of the United States stemmed partly from a belief current in America even before the Revolution that its people were destined for greatness. They were the people chosen to dominate and rule the North American continent. In the nineteenth century, this belief in the certain territorial expansion

of the United States would earn the name *manifest destiny*.

On a more practical note, the Mississippi River was an important trade route for the settlers west of the Appalachians. This region, known at that time as the American West or western frontier, had many rivers that flowed into the Mississippi, and Americans in Ohio, Kentucky, and Tennessee found it cheaper and easier to send crops and manufactured goods by water for sale in New Orleans in Louisiana than to cart them across the mountains to the Atlantic coast.

No problem existed in using the Mississippi's upper reaches because here it was an international waterway, with the United States on the eastern bank and

Spain on the western. But it was the lower stretch, below the mouth of the Red River, that was crucial since this part of the Mississippi was the route to the sea. However, both banks belonged to Spain because the eastern one was a part of Spanish Florida.

As long as Spain, or any other country, controlled navigation on the lower Mississippi, the water route could be closed at any time to American farmers and crafters. To make certain that this trade route stayed open, the U.S. government knew that eventually it would have to acquire at least southern Louisiana and western Florida.

KEEPING LOUISIANA SPANISH

American leaders such as Thomas Jefferson believed that, until the United States was strong enough to take part or all of Louisiana and Florida, these territories were best left in the hands of the Spanish. They felt that Spain would never be strong enough to resist a future American land grab. Jefferson and others were far less certain of America's ability to take these regions if they passed into the hands of the English or the French, both of whom were militarily much stronger than Spain.

Indeed, for early American leaders, the prospect of England in Louisiana and Florida was truly to be feared. British Canada already sat on America's northern border, and if the English took over Louisiana and regained Florida, they would then also have the land west and south of the United States. Great Britain

then, if it so desired, could literally box in the United States by putting its great fleet off the Atlantic coast, perhaps forcing the young nation to become once more an English territory.

But even without this bleak scenario, the presence of the British in Louisiana alone would almost certainly block U.S. expansion westward, as would repossession of Louisiana by France. Therefore, Alexander DeConde notes, "American leaders not only opposed any transfer of ownership [of Louisiana and Florida] from Spain, they also responded with alarm even to rumors of a change in status."[13] They could only hope that Spain would be strong enough to resist England or France but not the United States.

AMERICANS IN LOUISIANA

The federal government might not be ready to move into Louisiana, but any number of Americans were. Even as the United States was fighting its war of independence, its people were continuing to migrate west, pressing at and across the borders of Louisiana. In a 1779 letter to the Spanish governor of Louisiana, Thomas Jefferson wrote, "Notwithstanding the pressure of the present war [the Revolutionary War] on our people, they are lately beginning to extend their Settlements rapidly on the Waters of the Mississippi."[14]

Indeed, Gálveztown, the first American town in Louisiana, was founded by rebels fleeing from British-held Florida in 1779. Spain allowed other American refugees to find homes in Louisiana during the war,

REBEL AID

At the beginning of the Revolutionary War, Spain decided to provide aid to the American rebels. The Spanish government hoped to recover Florida from the British and thus sent the following order, reproduced at the website Americanrevolution.org, to the governor of Louisiana, Luis de Unzaga, in late 1776. Spain's insistence on secrecy was to avoid war with England.

"The King is informed regarding . . . the Americans' intentions delivered through General Charles Lee, major general and second in the American military command . . . to solicit [request] the establishment of systematic commerce with us and to inform that if in the event of the [American] seizure of Pensacola [Florida], as they are attempting, Your Majesty will be pleased to administer it [Pensacola]. . . . His Majesty commands . . . you [Unzaga] very secretly . . . [to assist] the Americans in their project to capture Pensacola and the other English settlements on the right bank of that River [the Mississippi]. . . .

In order to facilitate both objectives, you will be receiving . . . the weapons, munitions, clothes and quinine [medicine for malaria] which the English colonists [the Americans] ask and the most . . . secretive means will be established by you in order that you may supply these secretly with the appearance of selling them to private merchants, to which . . . secret instructions will be sent and some business person that may serve as contact.

Corresponding secret information is given to the governor of . . . Havana . . . that he will receive various items, weapons and other supplies that he will be sending to you without delay and that also he may send you then the surplus [gun]powder available in that Plaza [Havana] . . . and whatever muskets might be in that same Plaza."

only insisting that they take an oath of allegiance to the Spanish monarchy.

PROTECTING LOUISIANA

After the peace of 1783, Americans became less welcome as the possessive attitude of the United States toward Louisiana became clear to Spanish authorities. Spain had never been enthusiastic about taking over Louisiana because its obvious poverty meant that it would cost far more to run than it would earn. However, Louisiana formed a large physical barrier between the English colonies, and later

The Directory's Bid for Louisiana

In 1795 the Directory, the executive council that ran France, was trying to hammer out a treaty with Spain and hoped to insert a clause for the return of Louisiana. The French ambassador to Spain was given the following instructions, reprinted in E. Wilson Lyon's Louisiana in French Diplomacy. *The treaty effort failed, but Spain would remember the Directory's arguments and look favorably on Napoléon's later request for Louisiana.*

"The Directory holds . . . to the actual retrocession [the return] of Louisiana . . . , and even the interest of Spain commands it. . . .

[Spain] recognizes that the safety of Mexico demands that the French nation place itself on the Mississippi. It is the only way of guaranteeing Spanish North America, both from England, who covets [desires] this superb territory, and from the United States, where she exercises today an influence almost as great as before their independence and whose population increases with a rapidity truly disturbing for her neighbors. Yet . . . [Spain] refuses to put us in this post [position] . . . at the very time when New Spain [Mexico] runs the greatest danger; . . . [Spain] takes from us the means of turning to the defense of Mexico the old and profound attachment that the inhabitants of Louisiana . . . [have] retained for . . . [its] mother country, an attachment shared by the savages [Native Americans]. . . .

Do not keep from . . . [Spain] that the retrocession of Louisiana alone is able, by the advantages [food and supplies] which the French colonies will draw from it . . . , to compensate for the obligations that the treaty imposes on us for the defense and guarantee [of safety] of the numerous Spanish possessions."

the United States, and Spain's very valuable silver mines in the North American southwest. Without this buffer, Americans might be tempted to attack and perhaps seize those mines.

The Spanish would have liked to bar U.S. citizens from entering Louisiana at all, for as long as Americans remained in the United States, they posed no threat.

However, it was impossible to shut the borders of Louisiana. There were just too many miles, most of them wilderness, leading one Spanish official to remark, "You can't lock up an open field."[15]

The northern half of the colony was wide open to anyone since there were almost no troops in the area and indeed few Spaniards of any sort. The southern part of

Louisiana was better garrisoned with soldiers, but there were only about a thousand of them to patrol almost as many miles of river as well as keep order in New Orleans.

Spain, therefore, looked to other means to protect its colony. Like the French before them, the Spaniards recruited Native American allies, who attacked American pioneers, slowing their expansion toward and into Louisiana. Beginning in 1786, one Spanish recruit, the Creek chieftain Alexander McGillivray, whose father had been a Scottish trader, led a three-year attack against the American frontier from Kentucky to Georgia. This Creek war caused much damage and loss of life but failed to stop Americans from moving west.

ATTACKING U.S. UNITY

Spanish officials in Louisiana also spread the word that Spain would be happy to grant complete access to the lower Mississippi to any American territory that seceded—that is, broke away—from the United States. Such a region would have to join itself to Louisiana and its residents would have to become Spanish citizens. Authorities in Louisiana knew that Americans west of the Appalachians were often unhappy with the federal government, for the settlers felt that the United States was not doing enough to help them gain navigation rights along the lower Mississippi. Some of them even proposed that the American West secede.

However, Spain was unable to persuade American communities and territories to leave the United States. Most Americans, in whatever part of the country, despised the Spanish, whom they viewed as decadent and weak. Few western Americans seriously considered swapping U.S. rule for Spanish. Indeed, if the American West had seceded, it more likely would have launched an armed invasion of Louisiana than joined it peacefully.

AN ECONOMIC ATTACK

Along with its Indian and secession policies, Spain also tried an economic strategy. In 1784 it banned foreign traders from using the lower Mississippi and the port of New Orleans. Only Spanish merchants and Spanish ships were allowed entry.

American farmers in Ohio, Kentucky, and Tennessee were outraged by this act. It was not just being cut off from their market that angered them, though. They believed that they had been denied their natural right: access down the Mississippi to New Orleans, even though the city and part of the river belonged to another nation.

The people of Louisiana were also unhappy with the trade ban since most of the goods they bought, and practically all of their food, came from America. Thus, as DeConde writes,

> Spain's economic policy did not work out as desired, mainly because the people of Louisiana needed American goods and services and connived [schemed] at smuggling to get them. . . . Even the . . . municipal [city] council . . .

in New Orleans became a party to this illegal trade. It imported American flour. . . . Without the easily available American supply, people in the city might starve.[16]

TRADE AGREEMENTS

The trade ban was eventually lifted, and in 1788 a royal decree gave Americans the right to ship to and sell goods in New Orleans if they paid a 15 percent import-export tax, or duty, on these goods. Seven years later, even this duty was removed when Spain and the United States

Thomas Pinckney was instrumental in negotiating the Treaty of San Lorenzo with Spain, which allowed Americans to sell their products in New Orleans duty free.

signed the Treaty of San Lorenzo, also known as Pinckney's Treaty in honor of its American negotiator, Thomas Pinckney. In addition to guaranteeing New Orleans as a duty-free port, the treaty gave Americans the right to navigate the lower Mississippi. Spain also agreed to stop provoking Indian attacks against the United States.

The duty-free guarantee was to continue for three years. Then, Spain promised either to renew the provision for New Orleans or to provide another duty-free port on the Mississippi.

THE AMERICAN TIDE

Although Spain signed the Treaty of San Lorenzo in 1795, the Spanish took three years before honoring the treaty's terms. This delay much annoyed western Americans, who complained bitterly to the U.S. government about the holdup. There was continued talk of the western territories leaving the United States and then invading and taking over both Louisiana and western Florida.

As always, nothing came of this secession talk, for even without the Treaty of San Lorenzo, Americans were having their way in Louisiana. By the end of the eighteenth century, the Spanish colony was taking on a definite American flavor because of the number of U.S. citizens living and doing business in the territory. Over three thousand Americans a year passed through New Orleans, and the supposedly Spanish settlement of Baton Rouge, north of New

NAVIGATION AND TRADE

In the 1795 Treaty of Friendship, Limits, and Navigation, also known as the Treaty of San Lorenzo, which is excerpted from the website of the Avalon Project, Spain guaranteed Americans the right to navigate the lower Mississippi and to store goods at New Orleans without duty for three years and it agreed to stop inciting Native American attacks in U.S. territory.

"Article IV: It is . . . agreed that the western boundary of the United States, which separates them from the Spanish colony of Louisiana, is in the middle of the . . . bed of the river Mississippi from the northern boundary of the said states to the . . . thirty-first degree of latitude north of the equator. And His Catholic Majesty has likewise agreed that the navigation of the said river, in its whole breadth [length] from its source to the ocean, shall be free only to his subjects and the citizens of the United States. . . .

Article V: . . . Spain will not suffer her Indians to attack the citizens of the United States, nor the Indians inhabiting their [U.S.] territory. . . .

Article XII: . . . His Catholic Majesty will permit the citizens of the United States for the space of three years from this time to deposit their merchandise and effects [goods] in the port of New Orleans, and to export them from thence without paying any other duty than a fair price for the hire of the stores [storage], and his Majesty promises . . . to continue this permission . . . , or he will assign to them [the Americans], on another part of the banks of the Mississippi, an equivalent establishment."

Orleans on the Mississippi, had a government composed solely of Americans. Likewise, the majority of Louisiana land grants were being given to U.S. citizens.

Permanent American residents in Louisiana were supposed to swear their loyalty to Spain. However, few of those taking the oath gave it more than lip service. They remained Americans and, even more than ever, viewed Louisiana as an extension of America.

Even most of the trade into New Orleans was American. Every year hundreds of U.S. flatboats arrived loaded with cargoes of whiskey, tobacco, flour, nails, and a host of other goods. Half of the ships putting into the port were American, and even many of those flying the Spanish flag were owned by U.S. citizens. The thriving fur trade passing through St. Louis was also controlled by Americans.

NOTHING BUT TROUBLE

Spain was clearly losing control of Louisiana, although there were by no means enough Americans in the region to take over the colony. Still, the Spanish authorities in Louisiana were very upset by the American invasion and fired off a stream of requests for help from the home government.

However, these requests fell on increasingly deaf ears, for Spain was very tired of the whole Louisiana mess, which was costing it dearly. True, money was now flowing in Louisiana, but most of it was made by smuggling and therefore little of it was reaching the Spanish treasury. Indeed, Spain routinely spent about eight times as much to run the colony as it took in. Marshall Sprague observes that, as the eighteenth century drew to a close, the Spanish authorities felt more than ever that Louisiana was

> a troublesome liability. . . . The cost of owning the province was staggering. Its imports far exceeded its exports. . . . The cost of feeding, housing, and preserving the health of a soldier in Louisiana was five times higher than in Spain. . . . Here was a Spanish empire with nothing Spanish about it except a handful of civil servants, army officers, priests and nuns. . . . [The] non-Spanish majority conspired incessantly [constantly] to get free.[17]

DISPOSING OF LOUISIANA

Thus, by 1800, after suffering almost thirty years of draining expense and aggravation with Americans, Spain was anxious to rid itself of this trouble spot. However, the Spanish would not just give Louisiana away to anyone. Spain wanted to exchange it for something of value and also to ensure that a friendly power would occupy the region so that Louisiana would remain a barrier between the profitable Spanish southwest and the aggressive American nation.

Of the three nations most interested in Louisiana—the United States, Great Britain, and France—America was clearly out. England was not much better, being Spain's traditional colonial rival and enemy and just as likely as the Americans to try and seize the southwest territory. Only France, another Catholic country and Spain's historic ally in European affairs, would do as a North American neighbor. And, in fact, the French were very anxious to regain Louisiana.

THE FRENCH REVOLUTION

There were those in France who had always regretted the loss of Louisiana, and in Louisiana, many of those of French descent, known as Creoles, had always desired the return of French rule. However, until the last decade of the eighteenth century, the French government was not actively behind such schemes. Then, according to James K. Hosmer, "as the eigh-

A scene from the French Revolution, which attempted to bring about social, political, and economic change for all levels of society in France.

teenth century drew on, France tried repeatedly to recover what she began to feel had been too inconsiderately [thoughtlessly] given up."[18]

France of the 1790s was not the France at the end of the French and Indian War. That former France had been an absolute monarchy, where the king's word was law. In 1789 the French Revolution had erupted, sweeping aside the old political order and replacing it with a republican form of government modeled in part on the United States. The revolution's course was far from peaceful, and during the next five years, thousands were executed, including King Louis XVI and his queen,

Marie-Antoinette. Thousands more fled into exile.

In the years following the revolution, the new French Republic struggled to find a workable system of administering the country. Its attempts ranged from the dictatorial revolutionary government, responsible for most of the executions, to the Directory, an executive body of five individuals. In November 1799 the government came into the hands of Napoléon Bonaparte, who overthrew the Directory and became first consul of France. Eventually he declared France an empire and himself emperor.

THE FRENCH EMPIRE

Even before Napoléon's coup, France had started building a European empire by conquering Belgium and much of Italy. This war of conquest, however, began as a war of defense. In 1792 the French monarchy was officially abolished and the first republic took its place. Fearing that revolutionary France's republican ideals would spread, other European countries, most notably Great Britain and Austria, attacked France. Even Spain joined this alliance, which

After taking control of France, Napoléon Bonaparte wanted to rebuild the French Empire in North America.

hoped to restore the French monarchy. The alliance failed in its goal. Instead of going down in defeat, French armies poured across their borders to take the war to their neighbors. It was during the Italian campaign of 1796 that Napoléon first achieved military fame.

Napoléon would continue these conquests until he had brought most of Europe, excluding Great Britain and Russia, into the French Empire. But the first consul also had international goals. He wanted to rebuild as much of the former French domain in North America as possible. To do so, he needed Louisiana. Thus, in 1800 he began negotiations with Spain, which in 1796 had changed sides in the ongoing European war and was once more allied with France.

AN AGREEMENT IS REACHED

Actually, Spain had come close to working out a return of Louisiana to France a few years earlier. However, the French Directory was unable to provide a satisfactory piece of real estate in exchange for the North American colony. Additionally, as E. Wilson Lyon writes, the Spanish "feared that the Directory intended to cede [give] Louisiana to England as a price for peace,"[19] as indeed it did.

By July 1800, when Napoléon dispatched his envoy General Louis-Alexandre Berthier to Spain, Spanish officials were once more interested in dumping Louisiana. Napoléon, for his part, also hoped to add Florida to the deal, for he believed that Louisiana-Florida would be a base from

THE TREATY OF SAN ILDEFONSO

The 1800 Treaty of San Ildefonso, which is found on the Avalon Project website, returned Louisiana to France and gave the French six Spanish warships. In exchange, the Spanish king's brother-in-law, the duke of Parma, received an Italian kingdom. Although the treaty terms required that the rulers of both nations ratify the document within a month, Spain's Carlos IV took two years to accept the pact.

"Article 1: The French Republic undertakes to procure for His Royal Highness the . . . Duke of Parma an aggrandizement [expansion] of territory which should increase the population of his domains . . . , with the title of King and with all the rights which attach to the royal dignity; and the French Republic undertakes to obtain in this regard the assent [approval] of His Majesty the Emperor and King [of Austria] and other states. . . .

Article 2: The aggrandizement to be given to His Royal Highness the Duke of Parma may consist of Tuscany . . . or of any other . . . provinces of Italy which form a rounded [complete] state.

Article 3: His Catholic Majesty [the king of Spain] promises and undertakes on his part to retrocede [return] to the French Republic, six months after the full and entire execution of the above conditions and provisions regarding His Royal Highness the Duke of Parma, the colony or province of Louisiana. . . .

Article 5: His Catholic Majesty undertakes to deliver to the French Republic . . . six ships of war in good condition [each] built for seventy-four guns, armed and equipped and ready to receive French crews and supplies. . . .

The ratification of these . . . articles shall be . . . exchanged within the period of one month, . . . counting from the day of the signature of the present treaty."

---

which to attack English holdings in both Canada and the Caribbean.

Napoléon had a great admirer in the Spanish king, Carlos IV. But even more importantly, Carlos's queen, Maria Luisa, wished to see her brother, Fernando, the duke of Parma, with a kingdom of his own. Thus, the Spanish government proposed to swap Louisiana for one of the Italian states under French control. France would also ensure that other European powers recognized Parma as this region's legitimate ruler. In exchange, Spain would give France Louisiana, but not Florida, and six warships for the French fleet.

On October 1, 1800, the negotiators for both nations finalized the Treaty of San Ildefonso. The core of the treaty was article three, in which

> His Catholic Majesty [Carlos] promises and engages himself to retrocede [return] to the French Republic, six months after the full and entire execution of the above stipulations [requirements] relative to His Royal Highness, the Duke of Parma, the Colony or Province of Louisiana, with the same extent [area] that it now has in the hands of Spain and that it had when France possessed it.[20]

An additional agreement was required from the French, one that, although not written into the treaty, was of extreme importance to Spain. DeConde reports that Napoléon verbally "promised Carlos that France would not sell, give, or otherwise dispose of Louisiana to any third country."[21]

Both the negotiation and the treaty itself were kept secret. Napoléon and Carlos each feared that, if the United States got wind of the impending transfer of Louisiana, America would send in its army to take over the colony before the French could bring in sufficient troops to prevent such an act.

But rumors about the French-Spanish deal began flying almost immediately. The United States, ever sensitive about a change in ownership of Louisiana, began asking hard questions of French and Spanish diplomats and officials. How to handle the situation when the truth behind these rumors finally emerged fell to the newly elected third president of the United States, Thomas Jefferson.

3 The Louisiana Crisis

It was not until late November 1801 that the American government saw a copy of the Treaty of San Ildefonso when Rufus King, U.S. minister to Great Britain, for-

Thanks to the Louisiana Purchase, the United States nearly doubled in size under the presidency of Thomas Jefferson.

warded it from London. But long before then, the United States had concluded that the rumors concerning France's takeover of Louisiana were true. As early as May, King reported that the English were convinced that the colony would soon belong to France. Furthermore, articles in French newspapers bragged about the recovery of Louisiana, and Paris booksellers were doing a brisk business peddling books about the region.

Thus, for the United States, the worst had happened, and the crisis was at hand. Louisiana was going to change ownership, and its new landlords, the French, had the most powerful army in Europe, perhaps the world. The United States, and specifically its new president, Thomas Jefferson, had to decide on the best way of saving Louisiana for America.

JEFFERSON THE POLITICIAN

Jefferson was no newcomer to politics or crisis. A man of many interests and much talent, his public career had begun with the Revolutionary War when, as a member of the Second Continental Congress, he had helped draft the Declaration of

Independence in 1776. Since then, he had served as U.S. minister to France, as the first secretary of state under George Washington, as vice president under John Adams, and now, finally in 1801, as president, being inaugurated on March 4.

Jefferson was also a leader of and often vocal spokesman for the Democratic-Republican Party, the direct ancestor of the present-day Democratic Party and one of the first two American political parties, the other being the Federalists. The Republicans, as they were often known, advocated a strict reading of the U.S. Constitution and favored strong state governments over the national government. The Federalists, on the other hand, stood for a looser interpretation of the articles of the Constitution and for a forceful central government, to whose authority states submitted.

FREEDOM NEEDS ROOM

The Louisiana crisis was a painful one for President Jefferson. He was a great admirer of France and all things French, partly because of French aid during the Revolution and partly because of the intellectual excitement he had felt in Paris while minister to France.

However, Jefferson had to push his feelings aside, for he was also fully committed to the idea of American expansion. In an 1801 letter, Jefferson wrote that "it is impossible not to look forward to distant times, when our rapid multiplication will expand itself . . . [to] cover the whole northern . . . continent . . . with a people speaking the same language, governed in similar forms [ways], and by similar laws."[22] Marshall Sprague points out that for Jefferson, national expansion and individual freedom were linked:

> Jefferson . . . believed that farmers on their own land were the freest of men and . . . that a nation of farmers was superior to a nation of merchants . . . who tended to be enslaved and corrupted by the tyranny and materialism of money. Farmers needed more space as they became more numerous. . . . That was why he believed that possession of Louisiana and everything beyond it . . . to the Pacific would be necessary to complete development of the ideal republic that he had in mind when he wrote the Declaration of Independence.[23]

ENVOYS, ALLIANCES, AND THREATS

If at all possible, Jefferson preferred a peaceful solution to the Louisiana crisis. He would seek first to keep the colony in Spanish hands, and if that failed, he would try to buy New Orleans. Underneath these proposals would be the threat of war. Rufus King described this policy as offering France a choice between iron and gold—that is, the rod and the coin.

Jefferson's envoy to Napoléon was aristocratic New Yorker Robert R. Livingston, the newly appointed U.S. minister to France. Along with Jefferson, Livingston had been part of the committee that had written the Declaration of Independence. He had later served as secretary of foreign affairs prior to the adoption of the Constitution. Like the president, and despite being unable to speak French, Livingston much admired France.

In September 1801 Livingston received his instructions. If the transfer of Louisiana was not yet a fact, the minister was to voice American opposition to such a handover. If the transfer had already occurred, Livingston was to offer to buy New Orleans and the western part of Florida, which Jefferson, still ignorant of the terms of the Treaty of San Ildefonso, thought might be included in the French-Spanish deal. However, if Florida were still in Spanish hands, then Livingston was to seek French help in persuading Spain to sell its western region to the United States.

The minister was to make it very clear to the French that the United States would

As the U.S. minister to France, Robert R. Livingston was the chief negotiator in the U.S. attempt to acquire Louisiana.

PRESIDENTIAL CONCERNS

In an April 18, 1802, letter found in Major Presidential Decisions, *President Thomas Jefferson explains to the U.S. minister to France, Robert Livingston, what must happen if the French take control of Louisiana.*

"The cession [turnover] of Louisiana . . . by Spain . . . completely reverses all the political relations of the U.S. . . . Of all nations . . . France is the one which hitherto has offered the fewest points on which we could have any conflict of right, and the most points of communion of interest [common interest]. From these causes we have ever looked to her as our *natural friend*. . . . There is on the globe one single spot, the possessor of which is our natural and habitual enemy. It is New Orleans, through which the produce of three-eighths of our [national] territory must pass to market. . . . France placing herself in that door assumes to us the attitude of defiance. Spain might have retained it quietly for years. . . . Her feeble state would induce [cause] her to increase our facilities there, . . . and it would not perhaps be long before some circumstance might arise which might make the cession of it [New Orleans] to us [worthwhile]. . . . Not so can it ever be in the hands of France. . . . The energy . . . of her character, placed in a point of eternal friction with us, . . . these circumstances render it impossible that France and the U.S. can continue long friends when they meet in so irritable a position. . . . The day that France takes possession of N. Orleans . . . fixes the sentence. . . . It seals the union of two nations [the United States and England] who can maintain exclusive possession of the ocean. From that moment we must marry ourselves to the British fleet and nation."

not stand by and watch Louisiana change ownership. America would fight to take over the territory if that were necessary. As a mark of U.S. desperation and determination in this matter, Jefferson and his cabinet were even ready to seek British aid in such a war, a fact that Livingston was to stress in his discussions with the French. In London, Rufus King had already determined that the English did not want Napoléon in Louisiana and that, therefore, they might help the United States capture New Orleans, with Americans attacking by land and the British by sea.

THE KINGDOM OF ETRURIA

When Livingston arrived in France on November 10, the Treaty of San Ildefonso was over a year old, yet Louisiana remained under Spanish authority because Carlos IV of Spain had yet to sign the agreement. Napoléon, at first, was not bothered by Carlos's slowness since Louisiana would not be turned over to France until the duke of Parma had his Italian kingdom. The first consul planned to give the duke the central Italian grand duchy of Tuscany, which had a rich cultural history dating from the Renaissance and included the city of Florence, among many others.

Although French forces occupied the grand duchy, which the first consul renamed the Kingdom of Etruria, Napoléon wanted formal acknowledgment that the territory belonged to France and thus could be disposed of in any way France wished. Napoléon obtained that acknowledgment in a peace treaty with Austria on February 9, 1801.

A month later, Napoléon suggested some changes to the Treaty of San Ildefonso. First, since he despised Fernando, the duke of Parma, but approved of Fernando's son Luis, the first consul proposed that the son, and not the father, become king of Etruria. Second, Napoléon requested again that Florida be turned over to France along with Louisiana. Carlos was willing enough to have Luis, rather than Fernando, rule Etruria, but he flatly refused to part with Florida. Instead, France was to receive the Mediterranean island of Elba.

PEACE WITH BRITAIN

Napoléon's next objective was to arrange a peace with Great Britain, now the only country still at war with France. The French ruler believed that England was much less likely to interfere with French occupation of Louisiana in peacetime. The British, for their part, were tired of fighting after almost a decade of war, and the two countries signed the Peace of Amiens on October 1, 1801.

With Britain out of the way for the time being, the first consul was close to putting his ambitious plans for Louisiana in motion. Alexander DeConde observes that

> [the] articles of peace . . . freed him [Napoléon] from the menace of the British fleet. . . . He planned first to garrison the province [Louisiana] and then to populate and use it as a granary [grain storehouse] for France's islands in the Caribbean. He hoped his plan would end the dependence of those islands, as well as Louisiana, on the United States for food . . . and make them less vulnerable than in the recent past to blockade in time of war. This design . . . also assumed that once Louisiana had become . . . prosperous it would be able to defend itself even if cut off . . . by a hostile naval power such as England.[24]

The fear of a blockade at the Mississippi's mouth while Louisiana was building its strength was the major reason Napoléon wanted Florida. Whereas a small number of enemy ships could easily isolate New Orleans, even a large fleet would not be able to keep ships with supplies from landing somewhere along the four-hundred-mile Florida coast. These supplies could then be carted overland to

Louisiana. Thus, Napoléon was not happy with Spain's repeated refusal to give him Florida.

SANTO DOMINGO

In the fall of 1801, the ruler of France was also unhappy with the Spanish king's failure to sign the Treaty of San Ildefonso. Until Spain officially surrendered Louisiana, France could not occupy the colony. Napoléon demanded a signed treaty, pointing out that Luis was now king of Etruria. Spanish officials countered that France had only fulfilled part of its treaty obligations. The French had yet to obtain recognition of Luis's rule from other European nations, particularly Austria and Great Britain. This exchange went on for months without producing a signed treaty.

Meanwhile, the first consul had another matter demanding his attention, this time in the Caribbean. Santo Domingo, the western third of the island of Hispaniola, had been the richest of France's holdings in the Western Hemisphere. It produced large quantities of sugar, coffee, cocoa, indigo, and cotton, which filled more than seven hundred ships a year. At the time of the French Revolution, two-thirds of France's foreign investment was tied up in this colony.

At this time, Santo Domingo was divided into plantations, which were owned and operated by French settlers; over 90 percent of the colony's five hundred thousand–plus population, however, were African slaves who worked the plantation fields. In August 1791 these slaves rose up and killed or

Under the leadership of Toussaint-Louverture, Haitian slaves were successful in driving the French off the island.

drove their white owners off the island. Three years later, France abolished slavery in Santo Domingo.

A former slave, Toussaint-Louverture, became the colony's ruler. Although he did not declare independence from France, he struck bargains with the United States and Britain, guaranteeing them most of the region's production.

TO RETAKE A COLONY

Napoléon wanted to bring Santo Domingo, which, since 1795, included the whole island of Hispaniola, once more under French domination. He considered that the colony's wealth would be as essential to France's New World empire as would be Louisiana. Therefore, as he waited for a signed Spanish treaty, he ordered his brother-in-law General Charles-Victor-Emmanuel Leclerc to gather together a force of over twenty thousand soldiers and sail to Santo Domingo and retake the island colony.

The Santo Domingo expedition left on December 14, 1801, and arrived at Santo Domingo six weeks later. It was attacked almost as soon as it landed, but in a series of battles, it beat back Toussaint-Louverture's army. In May 1802 Toussaint-Louverture surrendered to Leclerc when the latter pledged to make the island leader a general in the French army and to treat him like an honored guest. After a month, however, Leclerc had Toussaint-Louverture arrested and shipped back to France, where he died in prison a year later.

BATTLE AND DISEASE

The French were confident that, with Toussaint-Louverture out of the way and his army defeated, their victory was complete. Orders then arrived from Napoléon instructing Leclerc to force all of the Africans on Santo Domingo back into slavery. But when Leclerc attempted to carry out this task, he found himself confronted by a new army with new leaders. The fighting was fierce, and the French did not fare well, particularly since the fall of 1802 also brought a yellow fever epidemic.

Reinforcements were rushed to Santo Domingo, but they were too few and too late. The French simply did not have enough naval transports to ferry in sufficient numbers of troops to crush the Santo Domingo army. By the end of the year, French casualties stood at seventeen thousand, among them Leclerc, who had died of yellow fever on November 2.

LIVINGSTON AND TALLEYRAND-PÉRIGORD

The sailing of the Santo Domingo expedition aroused the suspicion of the newly arrived Robert Livingston. The U.S. minister was convinced that Leclerc was headed for Louisiana after Santo Domingo. Rufus King in London, however, had already written Secretary of State James Madison, assuring him and Jefferson that "whatever may be the intentions of France in respect to the occupation of Louisiana, that no part of the force . . . , which are going to Santo Domingo, will be employed for this purpose."[25]

On December 4 Livingston had his first meeting with France's minister of foreign affairs, Charles-Maurice de Talleyrand-Périgord. The latter was an aristocrat, an accomplished diplomat, and a political survivor, having successfully changed his beliefs to match those of each government in power since the French Revolution.

The French minister was as enthusiastic about a revived French colonial empire as Napoléon, and he had absolutely no intention of selling New Orleans or Florida, even if France had possessed it. Having

Dispatch from Santo Domingo

In the following letter, dated August 6, 1802, and appearing in Major Presidential Decisions, *General Charles-Victor-Emmanuel Leclerc writes Napoléon of the desperate plight of the French army in Santo Domingo, ravaged by both fierce war and malaria.*

"Death has wrought such frightful havoc among my troops that when I tried to disarm the North [of Santo Domingo] a general insurrection [revolt] broke out. . . .

Now, Citizen Consul [Napoléon], . . . if you wish to preserve San Domingo, send a new army, send above all money, and I assure you that if you abandon us to ourselves, as you have hitherto done, this colony is lost, and once lost, you will never regain it. . . .

What general could calculate on a mortality of four-fifths of his army. . . [and of being] left without funds as I have in a country where purchases are made only for their weight in gold. . . .

I have shown you my real position with the frankness of a soldier. . . . Since terror is the sole resource left me, I employ it. At [the Santo Domingan town of] Tortugà, of 450 rebels I had 60 hanged. . . .

Send me immediate reinforcements, send me money, for I am in a really wretched position. . . .

I shall serve you with the same zeal [as always] as long as my health permits me. It is now worse and I am no longer able to ride. Bear in mind you must send me a successor. I have no one here who can replace me in the critical situation in which the colony will be for some time."

---

spent two years in the United States, Talleyrand-Périgord knew exactly how Americans felt about Louisiana, and he had expected nothing but hostility when they learned about the transfer of ownership. Like Napoléon, he hoped to soothe American feelings by ensuring the U.S. navigation rights along the lower Mississippi and the use of New Orleans as a shipping port.

Stalled Negotiations

The first meeting between Livingston and Talleyrand-Périgord went badly, as most of their encounters would. The foreign affairs minister denied that Spain was planning to restore Louisiana to France, even as he contradicted himself by refusing to sell New Orleans to the United States.

The American minister was unable to make any progress with Talleyrand-Périgord, and in the spring of 1802, a frustrated Livingston tried to meet with Napoléon to present the American case directly to the French ruler. However, the American envoy received a sharp note from Talleyrand-Périgord saying that all negotiations must go through him, the French foreign minister, and not the first consul.

Livingston explored other avenues of impressing on France America's determination to keep Louisiana out of French hands. He became friends with François

Charles-Maurice de Talleyrand-Périgord, the French minister of foreign affairs who negotiated the sale of Louisiana to the United States.

de Barbé-Marbois, minister of the public treasury, and the old Revolutionary War hero Lafayette. But as the spring of 1802 turned to summer and then to fall, his mission remained stalled. Writing to Madison in September, Livingston stormed that "there never was a Government in which less could be done by negotiation than here."[26]

A KING'S SIGNATURE

While Livingston worked on, France finally gained ownership of Louisiana when, on October 15, 1802, Carlos of Spain signed the Treaty of San Ildefonso, two years after it had been drawn up. The signing had come only after the French ambassador to Spain reaffirmed that Napoléon would not let a third country have Louisiana. Luis still had not been recognized by other European nations as king of Etruria, but Spain decided to waive this requirement.

The French had already begun assembling men and supplies to take possession of Louisiana. Commanded by General Claude Victor, the Louisiana force was scheduled to sail on November 22 from Helvoë Sluys, a Dutch port near Rotterdam in the French-controlled Netherlands. However, on the date of departure, the expedition still lacked sufficient supplies, soldiers, and naval transports to set sail. French military resources were being monopolized by the disastrous campaign on Santo Domingo. Ships were a particular problem since the French simply did not have enough. As December gave way to January, Victor's command found itself trapped for the next two months as ice blocked the harbor of Helvoë Sluys.

TROUBLE AT NEW ORLEANS

Napoléon's grand plans for North America had run afoul of Spanish delays, determined Santo Domingo fighters, and bad weather. Yet, as far as the United States knew—even its envoy Livingston in Paris—all was well with France's Louisiana venture.

All was definitely and publicly not well in North America that fall of 1802. On October 16 Juan Ventura Morales, the acting intendant, or royal agent of the king of Spain, revoked the American right of deposit—that is, the right to store trade goods—on the wharfs or in the warehouses of New Orleans.

ENDING THE AMERICAN DEPOSIT

On October 16, 1802, Intendant Juan Ventura Morales issued a proclamation, reprinted in Major Presidential Decisions, *that ended the right of Americans to deposit, or store, goods duty free at New Orleans. Morales excuses his action because the time limit for the deposit had expired and because the reason for the deposit's existence had disappeared with the signing of the Treaty of Amiens and the end of war between Spain and England.*

"As long as it was necessary to tolerate the commerce of neutrals [in the war with England] which is now abolished, it would have been prejudicial [harmful] to the province [Louisiana] had the Intendant, in compliance with his duty, prevented the deposit in the city, of the property of Americans, granted to them by the twenty-second article of the Treaty of Friendship, Limits, and Navigation [the Treaty of San Lorenzo] . . . during the limited term of three years.

With the publication of the ratification of the Treaty of Amiens and the reestablishment of the communication between the English and Spanish subjects, that inconvenience [of American deposit] has ceased. . . . The twenty-second article of the said treaty takes from me the power of continuing the toleration which necessity required; since after the fulfillment of the said term [of three years], this Ministry can no longer consent to it [the deposit] without an express order of the King; therefore, . . . I order, that from this date, the privilege which the Americans had of importing and depositing their merchandise . . . in this capital [New Orleans], shall be interdicted [prohibited]."

Spain had the right to stop this deposit since more than three years had passed since the Treaty of San Lorenzo had gone into effect. However, the treaty required that an alternative port be found for American use. Morales brushed this provision aside, along with the entire treaty. The intendant claimed that Spain had been at war at the time of the pact and had meant the treaty to be simply a wartime measure designed to encourage trade with the neutral United States. Now that the European war was over, so was the need for the treaty.

Although western Americans could still sail down the Mississippi and load cargo from boats directly onto ships, they were as angry as if their trade had been stopped altogether. They believed that this ban was all part of the French takeover and that Napoléon had persuaded Spain to revoke the right of deposit. In fact, the first consul had recently agreed to honor American trading rights along the lower Mississippi, one of the few accomplishments Livingston so far had to show for his months of negotiation.

WAR THREATS AND DIPLOMACY

In the western territories, talk of war with Spain and of immediate seizure of Louisiana began. When news of Morales's act reached Washington, D.C., the cry for war was taken up in the newspapers and in Congress. The Federalists, who were the minority party in both houses, called for Jefferson to mobilize the army and the

Secretary of State James Madison was key in preventing war between the United States and Spain.

western militia, or volunteer units, and attack at once.

The Republican majority managed to vote down Federalist measures that would have forced the president to declare war, but Jefferson nonetheless instructed his secretary of war to begin military preparations. The president knew that war might be inescapable. Still, as usual, he hoped for a more peaceful solution. He therefore had Madison write to the U.S. minister in Spain, who was to ask the Spanish government to reinstate the right of Americans to deposit goods in New Orleans. Jefferson himself personally visited the Spanish minister to the United States, who agreed to write to Morales about restoring this right.

In December, Madison wrote to Livingston to see if the French would bring pressure on Spain. The secretary of state wanted Napoléon to know that the Mississippi River would soon be swarming with "200,000 militia [members] . . . , every man of whom would march at a moment's warning to remove obstacles from that outlet to the sea."[27]

A SURPRISING OFFER

In January, Jefferson decided to send a second envoy to France. His choice was James Monroe, a fellow Virginian who had attended law school with the president. Jef-

James Monroe was sent to France to assist in the acquisition of Louisiana.

ferson was confident that Livingston needed no help in negotiating with the French government, but because Monroe owned land in the West, the Virginian's presence in Paris would show westerners that the administration was taking their grievances seriously. By soothing western feathers, Jefferson believed he could keep the settlers from attacking Louisiana.

By the time Monroe arrived in Paris, on April 12, 1803, the deposit crisis was over. On March 1 Carlos IV had ordered Morales to restore the American right of deposit in New Orleans.

But an even more important development awaited Monroe. On April 11, the day before the new envoy's arrival, Talleyrand-Périgord had surprised Livingston by asking if the American minister thought the United States was prepared to purchase the entire territory of Louisiana. As Livingston wrote to Madison later that day, "I told him it was a subject that I had not thought of; but that I supposed we should not object to twenty million [francs]. . . . He told me this was too low an offer and that he would be glad if I would reflect upon it."[28]

NAPOLÉON'S CHANGE OF MIND

Talleyrand-Périgord's unexpected offer to Livingston reflected an equally unexpected change of mind by Napoléon. In March the first consul told his advisers that he was abandoning Louisiana and his plans for a French empire in North America. Instead, he would sell the territory to the United States.

Several factors influenced this decision. The Santo Domingo rebels had thoroughly beaten the French army, and the island was lost to France. French forces on Santo Domingo would surrender on November 9, 1803, and less than two months later, on January 1, 1804, the islanders would declare their independence and rename their home Haiti.

The French campaign on Santo Domingo had squandered money, troops, and supplies, much of which had originally been destined for Louisiana. And the first consul was going to need all three soon because the peace with the British was breaking apart, and it was clear that both nations would soon be at war again. By selling Louisiana, Napoléon would be able to raise some much needed cash with which to finance that looming war.

Ironically, the peace was crumbling in part because the British were upset by the buildup of French forces at Helvoë Sluys. When the ice that had kept General Victor and his command from sailing melted in early March, the British blockaded the port. The English were not at all convinced that these troops were headed for Louisiana since this Dutch harbor was also an excellent point from which to launch an invasion of England.

STAYING FRIENDS WITH AMERICA

But perhaps the most compelling reason for Napoléon's backing away from Louisiana was his need to stay on good terms with the United States. The Jefferson administration had convinced Napoléon that the United

States would attack Louisiana if the French moved into the colony in force. And, in the coming war with Britain, France would fare better with a friendly, rather than hostile, United States. An America at war with France over Louisiana could well ally itself with England. E. Wilson Lyon observes that,

useful as the purchase price might have been, reasons of strategy rather than finance determined the reversal in policy in regard to Louisiana. Napoleon's primary motive was to break up the growing Anglo-American *rapprochement* [growing together] and to secure the good will of the United States for France. . . . The vast shipping interests of a neutral United States would be of great assistance in the war with England. What were a malaria infested town [New Orleans] . . . and a vast unexplored wilderness in comparison with the friendship of the second maritime [seagoing] power of the world in a struggle with the first? It would have been better to forsake the Colony entirely rather than by its retention force the United States into an alliance with England.[29]

Napoléon was convinced that if France went to war with Britain, it would not be able to hold Louisiana for more than sixty days. Even without an American-English alliance, to keep Louisiana would still see France at war with the United States. In a war for Louisiana, the United States could easily put large numbers of troops across the Mississippi and into the colony. France, on the other hand, would have to ship its soldiers overseas. Then, once in Louisiana, the French would have to defend a territory that could not even feed itself without supplies from the very country attacking it.

So, since France was likely to lose Louisiana anyway, it might as well sell it to the United States and reap financial and political benefits. To Talleyrand-Périgord, Napoléon said, "I will not keep a possession that will not be safe in our hands. . . . I shall make it serve me . . . to attach them [the Americans] to me."[30]

The goodwill of the United States was thus worth much to Napoléon. He was even willing to break his word—given twice—to Spain that he would not let the territory pass into the hands of a third na-tion; the first consul saw no advantage in returning the land to Spain, a country whose national interests already bound it to France. Additionally, selling Louisiana was revenge against Spain for its delays in the signing of the Treaty of San Ildefonso and for its refusal to give up Florida, actions that Napoléon believed had contributed to the failure of his Louisiana venture.

The Sale of Louisiana

Monroe was as amazed and pleased at the sudden turn of events as Livingston. Their only problem was that neither had authority to negotiate for the entirety of Louisiana.

Napoléon discusses the details of the Louisiana Purchase Treaty with Talleyrand-Périgord and Finance Minister Barbé-Marbois.

Indeed, Monroe had been given only $2 million, which he brought with him to France, and he was instructed to offer no more than $9 million for New Orleans and Florida. The asking price for Louisiana was certain to exceed that amount.

Still, without any other means of communicating with Washington except by sailing across the Atlantic Ocean, there was no time to consult their superiors. Neither man wished to give the French time to reconsider and thus lose this opportunity. With or without authorization, Livingston and Monroe had to sit down with the French and hammer out a treaty for the sale of Louisiana.

On May 2, after only three weeks of bargaining between the two American envoys and Finance Minister Barbé-Marbois, who had replaced Talleyrand-Périgord as the French negotiator, the Louisiana Purchase Treaty was finished. The three negotiators then signed the pact and postdated it April 30. Three weeks later, Napoléon ratified, or approved, the treaty on May 22, four days after war resumed between France and England.

There were still hurdles ahead before Louisiana belonged to America. The U.S. Senate had to ratify the treaty by October 30, 1803, only six months away. But, more importantly, although Louisiana was technically French territory until the treaty became effective, the colony was in reality still occupied by Spain. How the Spanish government would react would determine the ease or difficulty of U.S. possession of Louisiana.

4 Taking Possession

On July 3, 1803, Thomas Jefferson learned of the completed Louisiana Purchase Treaty from Rufus King, who was back from London. The president was jubilant. His envoys had bought the whole of Louisiana for $15 million, less than twice

In July 1803 Rufus King (pictured) informed Thomas Jefferson that the United States had purchased Louisiana.

what the president had been prepared to pay for a single city and a part of Florida. Best of all, Jefferson's insistence on diplomacy over war had given the United States this huge region without bloodshed. As the Washington-based *National Intelligence* newspaper wrote five days later, "We have secured our rights [to Louisiana] by pacific [peaceful] means."[31]

The president and the newspaper were being premature in their celebration since America's hold on Louisiana was far from secure. Indeed, despite the treaty, the United States could still find itself in a war over the territory. Even as the treaty was making its way across the Atlantic, Napoléon was regretting his hasty decision to sell the colony. Additionally, Spain was protesting that the sale was illegal and was threatening to keep its troops in Louisiana, treaty or no treaty.

THE TREATY

The actual treaty arrived in Washington on July 14, and Jefferson and his cabinet had their first look at what Livingston and Monroe had worked out. The purchase gave the United States title to the

THE TREATY

The Louisiana Purchase Treaty, actually titled the Treaty Between the United States of America and the French Republic, which is reproduced in James K. Hosmer's The History of the Louisiana Purchase, *may have sold all of Louisiana to the United States, but it also safeguarded the rights of the territory's settlers and Native Americans as well as protecting French and Spanish shipping interests.*

"Art. 1. . . . And whereas, in pursuance [the carrying out of] the Treaty [of San Ildefonso], particularly of the third article, the French Republic has an incontestible [undeniable] title to the domain [Louisiana], the First Consul of the French Republic [Napoléon], desiring to give to the United States a strong proof of friendship, doth hereby cede [give] to the said United States, in the name of the French Republic, forever . . . the said territory. . . .

Art. 2. In the cession made by the preceding article, are included the adjacent islands belonging to Louisiana, all public lots and squares, vacant lands, and all public buildings, fortifications, barracks, and other edifices [buildings], which are not private property. . . .

Art. 3. The inhabitants of the ceded territory shall be incorporated in the Union of the United States and admitted as soon as possible, according to the principles of the Federal Constitution, to the enjoyment of all rights . . . of citizens of the United States. . . .

Art. 6. The United States promises to execute such treaties . . . as may have been agreed between Spain and the . . . nations of Indians. . . .

Art. 7. . . . It has been agreed . . . that . . . French ships . . . and the ships of Spain . . . shall be admitted during a space of twelve years in the port of New Orleans . . . in the same manner as the ships of the United States. . . .

Art. 10. The present treaty shall be ratified [approved] . . . in the space of six months after the date of the signature. . . .

Done at Paris, . . . the 30th April, 1803."

whole of Louisiana, including all public buildings and property as well as all public records. There was no attempt to define the boundaries of the region. The treaty merely repeated wording from the Treaty of San Ildefonso, saying Louisiana was to have "the same extent that it now has in the hands of Spain and that it had when France possessed it [until 1762]."[32] Florida, which President

Jefferson, like Napoléon, wanted, was not included in the sale since it was still a Spanish colony.

Other terms guaranteed that, for twelve years, French and Spanish ships would be charged the same duties as American vessels at New Orleans. Current residents of the colony were to be given U.S. citizenship. And finally, the United States agreed to honor all existing treaties between Spain and Native Americans in Louisiana.

PAYING THE BILL

Two attached documents, known as conventions, described the financial arrangements. For 60 million francs ($11.25 million), the United States would have Louisiana. The American government also agreed to pay 20 million francs ($3.75 million) to American citizens owed money by France. This latter sum represented damage claims by Americans for ships and cargoes seized by French privateers during the European war of the 1790s. Thus, the total purchase price was 80 million francs or $15 million.

The first convention also laid out exactly how the United States was to pay France the $11.25 million for Louisiana since the nation did not have that much money on hand. American revenues at the time averaged $10 million a year, and the country had a national debt of $7 million. Therefore, to raise the money, the United States agreed to issue stock certificates to France, which would then sell the certificates to European banks so that

Napoléon could have immediate use of the money.

After the sale of the stocks, America would owe the banks, not France, an interest payment of 6 percent every six months and would have to finish buying back the certificates by 1821. In the end, the total interest paid by the United States turned out to be over $11 million, almost the selling price of Louisiana. But, even with this sum calculated into America's outlay for the region, the United States obtained Louisiana for around 5¢ per acre, still a bargain.

THE CONSTITUTIONAL ISSUE

The treaty now had to be ratified by the Senate, and the financial arrangements had to be approved by the House of Representatives. Because Congress was not due back until November, after the October 30 deadline set for ratification in the treaty's terms, Jefferson called for a special session to meet on October 17.

The president had one problem with the treaty: He believed it to be unconstitutional for the U.S. government to add territory to the country. Jefferson held to a strictly literal reading of the Constitution, and if some action were not specifically allowed, then it was forbidden. And, although the Constitution did have a provision for admitting new states, it did not mention territorial expansion at all. Jefferson was therefore firmly convinced that a constitutional amendment was necessary to make the purchase treaty legal.

The president had already raised this issue with his cabinet earlier in the year,

A Constitutional Issue

Even before the Louisiana Purchase, Thomas Jefferson worried that acquiring territory was unconstitutional. His attorney general, Levi Lincoln, was convinced that expansion was illegal, but in a memo dated January 13, 1803, and excerpted in Major Presidential Decisions, *Secretary of the Treasury Albert Gallatin argued that nothing in the Constitution prevented the United States from expanding.*

"Does any constitutional objection really exist?

The 3d section of the 4th Article of the Constitution provides:

1st. That new States may be admitted by Congress into this Union.

2d. That Congress shall have power to dispose of and make all needful [necessary] rules and regulations respecting the territory or other property belonging to the United States.

Mr. Lincoln . . . [supposes] that the new States . . . must be carved out of . . . territory [already] belonging to the United States; and . . . that the power given Congress of making regulations . . . is expressly confined to the territory *then* [at the ratification of the Constitution] belonging to the Union.

A general and perhaps sufficient answer is that the whole [of Lincoln's reasoning] rests on a supposition . . . [since there are] no words in the section [of the Constitution] which confines the authority given to Congress . . . ; whilst, on the contrary, the existence of the United States as a nation presupposes the power enjoyed by every nation of extending their territory by treaties, and the general power given to the President and the Senate of making treaties designates [indicates] the organs [offices] through which the acquisition may be made, whilst this section provides the proper authority [Congress] for either admitting in the Union or governing as subjects the territory thus acquired."

Secretary of the Treasury Albert Gallatin was in favor of the U.S. purchase of Louisiana.

when the territory in question was only New Orleans and western Florida. His attorney general, Levi Lincoln, had written a long response, basically agreeing with Jefferson's position.

However, Secretary of the Treasury Albert Gallatin wrote a memo countering Lincoln's. Gallatin reasoned that all countries recognized the right of nations to expand through treaties and that certainly the United States also enjoyed this right. And, since the Constitution gave the president, with Senate approval, the right to enter into any treaty, a treaty acquiring territory was certainly constitutional.

NAPOLÉON HAS SECOND THOUGHTS

Although most of the cabinet agreed with Gallatin, the president was not convinced. When the purchase treaty arrived, he immediately proposed tying its ratification in the Senate to a proposed amendment giving the president power to acquire territory. The cabinet disagreed. Such an amendment, the presidential advisers pointed out, would slow the ratification process since once the amendment passed through Congress, which might take some time, it had to be voted on by each state legislature. It would probably be impossible to amend the Constitution by the treaty's ratification deadline, a little over three months away at that time.

This deadline took on added weight when a message from Livingston arrived on August 17. According to the minister, Napoléon was having second thoughts

about the sale of Louisiana and would cancel the treaty if it were not ratified by October 30. Additionally, Livingston wrote, the treaty must be dealt with "without altering a syllable of the terms. . . . Be persuaded that France is sick of the bargain, . . . and the slightest pretense [change] will lose you the treaty."[33] In light of this information, Jefferson quickly put aside his constitutional qualms, deciding that an amendment could be sought after the treaty was safely ratified.

THE TREATY GOES TO THE SENATE

On October 17 Jefferson addressed both houses of Congress, explaining the importance of the treaty before them. But he made no mention at all of a constitutional amendment so as not to stir up any possible controversy that might delay ratification. At the end of the president's speech, the Senate began debating the merits of the Louisiana Purchase Treaty.

Popular opinion certainly supported the treaty and its passage, for most Americans approved of the purchase of Louisiana. Among the senators and representatives, all of Jefferson's fellow Republicans favored the treaty. The Federalists were less united in their support of the purchase. They were unhappy that the president and the Democratic-Republican Party would harvest the glory for having acquired Louisiana and thus profit politically from the deal. Still, many Federalists were as committed to U.S. expansion as their political foes; they had been urging for years—indeed, as recently as the New

Orleans deposit crisis—that the United States take Louisiana by force.

TREATY CRITICS

Other Federalists, both in and out of Congress, openly opposed the treaty. Even before October 17, these critics made their opposition abundantly clear in speeches, letters, and newspaper articles. Although Federalists believed in a strong presidency, Federalist critics ironically attacked Jefferson for exceeding his official powers by agreeing to buy Louisiana and by setting a price for that acquisition without consulting Congress. Other opponents feared that the eastern United States would become depopulated as Americans rushed west into the newly opened territory, and still others claimed that the United States was now too large to be governed democratically and that the country would eventually split apart.

But the harshest criticism was over the price to be paid. The *Boston Columbian Centinel* described Louisiana as "a great waste, a wilderness unpeopled with any beings except wolves and wandering Indians. . . . We are to give money of which we have too little for land of which we already have too much."[34] James K. Hosmer summarizes the feelings of Federalist critics over this financial burden:

> Fifteen million dollars! You can say it in a breath; you can write it in a few strokes. But what does it mean? Weigh it and there will be 433 tons of solid silver. It would take 866 wagons to draw it. The wagons in line would . . . stretch out 5 1/3 miles. If a man were to set out to fill the wagons, at the rate of 16 a day, it would take him 2 months. Pile up dollar [coin] on dollar, . . . the pile would be 3 miles high. . . . All the coin in the country, gold and silver, would fall far short of such a sum.[35]

CONGRESS ACTS

These objections and others were brought forth by Federalist senators during two days of heated debate over the Louisiana Purchase Treaty. Nothing, however, could stop ratification, which came in a vote on October 20 with twenty-four senators in favor and seven against. One Federalist complained that the Senate had taken less time to consider this major treaty than it did for one of the many small Indian contracts.

Not long after the Senate vote, the House overwhelmingly approved the financial arrangements contained in the treaty's two conventions. Additionally, the representatives authorized Jefferson to make all necessary preparations to take possession of Louisiana. And finally, they gave the president the power to appoint a temporary government to run the new territory.

A STRONGER FEDERAL GOVERNMENT

Jefferson was never to seek a constitutional amendment in connection with the Louisiana Purchase. He would later justify

The Louisiana Purchase Treaty was heavily debated by both houses of Congress before finally being ratified on October 20, 1803.

his disregard for a rigorous constitutional reading on the grounds that the good of the country came first: "To lose our country [now doubled and strengthened by Louisiana] by a scrupulous [exact] adherence to written law, would be to lose the law itself, . . . thus absurdly sacrificing the end to the means."[36] Despite this constitutional lapse, Jefferson tried to remain true to his political beliefs. Historian Gerhard Casper observes,

> There can be little question that, on the whole, Jefferson strove to abide by the letter and spirit of the Constitution. While he was the most force-

ful chief executive yet, he worried . . . about his accountability to the people whose agent he was. It was that agency relationship . . . that offered Jefferson the hope . . . of ultimate vindication [by the American people] for legal trespasses.[37]

Nonetheless, the president's willingness to buy territory—an act not mentioned in the Constitution—and the Senate's approval of that purchase, set two important precedents. First, some powers of the federal government were now recognized as implied—that is, presupposed to exist rather than baldly stated in writing. Second, in times of national need, the government could ignore the Constitution and take whatever action it thought necessary. The ultimate result was that the authority of the federal government was both broadened and strengthened.

A CLEAR TITLE TO LOUISIANA?

During the treaty debate in the House of Representatives, New York's Gaynor Griswold, a Federalist opponent of the purchase, demanded to see a copy of the Treaty of San Ildefonso as well as an official record showing that Spain had actually given France title to Louisiana. Griswold wanted proof that the territory was Napoléon's to sell. Otherwise, the United States might be paying $15 million for land still claimed by Spain.

Griswold did not get his proof because the Jefferson administration did not have it; despite this fact, the New York representative was unable to delay the House from approving the funds needed to pay for Louisiana until such proof was produced. However, his concern about France's right to sell the colony was valid, for even before

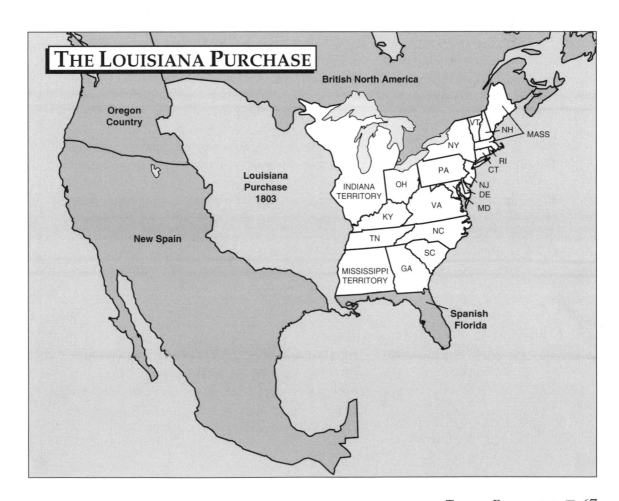

THE LOUISIANA PURCHASE

British North America

Oregon Country

New Spain

Louisiana Purchase 1803

INDIANA TERRITORY

OH

KY

TN

MISSISSIPPI TERRITORY

GA

VT

NH

MASS

NY

PA

RI

CT

NJ

DE

MD

VA

NC

SC

Spanish Florida

Congress began debating the purchase treaty and its conventions, Spain complained to the United States that France was trying to dispose of Spanish territory.

SPAIN PROTESTS

Spain's minister to the United States, Carlos Martinez de Irujo, explained to Secretary of State James Madison that Louisiana was not France's to sell. First, Napoléon had pledged not to pass the colony onto a third country, and accordingly, he had no right to offer the territory to America. Second, the Treaty of San Ildefonso between Spain and France required that the king of Etruria, Luis of Parma, be recognized by other European nations before France could take formal possession of Louisiana. Napoléon

A NOTE OF PROTEST

The Spanish government was very angry when it learned of the sale of Louisiana to the United States. In a September 27, 1803, note, appearing in Major Presidential Decisions, *Carlos Martinez de Irujo, Spanish minister to America, outlined for Secretary of State James Madison why France had no right to sell Louisiana nor the United States to buy it.*

"The King my master charges me again to remind the American Government that the . . . French Ambassador [to Spain] . . . , in the name of his Republic, . . . [swore] that France never would alienate [hand over] Louisiana, and . . . that the sale of this province to the United States is founded in the violation of a promise so absolute that it ought to be respected; a promise, without which the King my master would, in no manner, have dispossessed himself of Louisiana. His Catholic Majesty entertains too good an opinion of the character of . . . the Government of the United States . . . [and hopes] that it will suspend the ratification . . . of a treaty which rests on such a basis. There are other reasons. . . . France acquired . . . the retrocession [return] of Louisiana under obligations, whose entire fulfillment was absolutely necessary to give her complete right over the said province; such was that of causing the King of Tuscany [Etruria] to be acknowledged by the Powers of Europe; but . . . the French government has not procured [gained] this acknowledgment promised. . . . Under such circumstances it is evident that the treaty of sale entered into between France and the United States does not give the latter any right to acquire and claim Louisiana."

had completely failed to honor this treaty term. The French first consul's action and inaction had consequently voided the pact between Spain and France. Therefore, Irujo concluded, it followed that the Louisiana transaction between France and the United States was illegal because the territory was still a Spanish colony.

Madison responded by saying that France indeed did have title to Louisiana, for Carlos IV had signed over the land to the French in October of the previous year. Furthermore, any violation of the Treaty of San Ildefonso was a matter that concerned only the Spanish and French governments. And so, since the United States had acted in good faith, it had every intention of possessing Louisiana according to its treaty with France.

THREATS OF WAR

The American government might have been determined to possess Louisiana, but for all practical purposes Spain still controlled the region since only a handful of French officials and soldiers were in the colony. The remainder of the French occupation force had never left Europe, having been slated to sail with the canceled Victor expedition.

Spain, therefore, countered America's firm resolve to claim Louisiana with a threat of war. Irujo informed Madison that the Spanish government was prepared to send troops from Cuba, Mexico, and other colonies to reinforce Louisiana and to resist any attempt by the United States to take over the territory.

Madison told Jefferson that such Spanish opposition posed no serious problem to U.S. occupation of Louisiana. American military and militia units were already being mobilized, and if these units moved quickly, they could reach Louisiana before Spanish reinforcements and could easily swamp the undermanned garrisons of the colony. Moreover, Madison added, if Spain went to war over Louisiana, it would stand alone. Its ally, France, had already betrayed it in this matter. And Spain's only other possible source of aid, England, was pleased to see Louisiana in the hands of the Americans rather than France or Spain.

In the end, Spain opted to avoid a risky and costly war that most likely would have lost Louisiana anyway. Additionally, the Spanish also stood to lose Florida since Jefferson threatened to attack this colony if war broke out. Alexander DeConde writes that "Spanish policy makers . . . thought not only that resistance was useless but also that it [defeat] would deepen Spain's humiliation and bring more loss."[38] Ultimately, Spain embraced the Louisiana Purchase Treaty, recognizing it as a legal document.

FRANCE TAKES POSSESSION OF LOUISIANA

With the end of Spanish opposition, France was finally able to take official control of lower Louisiana. On November 30, a dark, rainy day, a French governor and council replaced the Spanish government of New Orleans. It was a somber affair, with one

American observer noting that the large crowd made not a single sound. During the next week, however, the silence of the ceremony gave way to parties and balls celebrating the change in ownership.

St. Louis and the rest of upper Louisiana was left in Spanish hands since the French would only hold the colony for a mere three weeks. French officials were mainly concerned with the impending arrival of the Americans, not with extending their authority through the whole of Louisiana.

At New Orleans, the new government attended to the basic needs of the city, with peace being kept by a combined force of Spanish troops and some one hundred American volunteers. The few French officers took command of Spanish forts along the lower Mississippi. Their responsibilities were light and short-lived.

William C. C. Claiborne was appointed the first American governor of the lower Louisiana Territory.

THE UNITED STATES IN LOUISIANA

On December 20, 1803, in New Orleans's Place d'Armes, a public square near the river, French authorities handed over lower Louisiana to its new American governor, William C. C. Claiborne. Accompanying Claiborne were General James Wilkinson and some 350 American troopers. Although a small force, it was sufficient to handle the less than 100 Spanish soldiers in New Orleans, if that had proven necessary.

The day was sunny, a fact that the Americans took as a good omen for their future in Louisiana. Claiborne spoke briefly, reassuring the French and Spanish residents that their rights, property, and religion would be respected. The crowd received these remarks in complete silence. Indeed, except for the Americans in the audience, the assembly, as it had three weeks before, remained quiet during the entire ceremony. A French botanist, C. C. Robin, described the scene:

> I saw the French flag slowly descending and that of the U.S. gradually rising at the same time. . . . The American flag remained stuck for a long time, . . . as if it were confused at taking the place of that [the French flag] to which it owed its glorious independence. . . . It was not until the [American] flag had been . . . hoisted

up that suddenly piercing cries of "Huzza" [a cheer] burst from the midst of . . . [the Americans], who waved their hats at the same time. Those cries and that movement made more gloomy the silence and quietness of the rest of the crowd.[39]

The somberness of the transfer ceremony was soon replaced by a party that began at three in the afternoon and lasted until nine the next morning. Dancing and gambling filled the New Orleans night.

The party goers toasted each other and the new owners of Louisiana.

THE LOUISIANA JUBILEE

The news of the successful—and peaceful—transfer of New Orleans and lower Louisiana from France to the United States reached Washington, D.C., on January 15, 1804; the next day the French received their stocks. Upper Louisiana had yet to be given over to American control,

The U.S. flag is raised over New Orleans on December 20, 1803, at the Place d'Armes as control of lower Louisiana transfers from France to the United States.

but it would be within a few weeks. No one feared that Spain would desire to hold on to this sparsely populated area, as it would not.

On January 27 the nation's capital became the site of the Louisiana Jubilee when the Republican members of Congress threw a lavish dinner party to honor Jefferson and his cabinet. Three cannons were fired repeatedly during the festivities, which were followed four days later by a ball for five hundred people. The jubilee spread to the rest of the country, with some places spending days, and even weeks, celebrating America's new possession.

Although the United States now owned the Louisiana Territory, it was not clear exactly what the nation had gained. The customs of the region's inhabitants were unknown to most Americans, its borders were not defined, and most of the land was unexplored. The United States had a great deal of work ahead of it to make Louisiana a part of the Union.

Chapter

5 Exploration, Conspiracy, and War

On March 9, 1804, Captain Amos Stoddard took possession of the northern portion of Louisiana for the United States at a small ceremony held at St. Louis. Stoddard had to hand the region over to himself since the day before he had acted as an agent for France in receiving northern Louisiana from Spain, the French not having bothered with the upper reaches of the territory during their brief ownership.

Now the United States officially had it all, and the young nation faced the challenge of making Louisiana a part of itself. America had a job ahead of it to govern

St. Louis became the capital of the northern Louisiana Territory in 1805, a short time after Congress divided the area into two jurisdictions.

the vast territory, explore its lands, and determine and defend its borders.

AN AMERICAN COLONY

On March 26, 1804, Congress voted to split Louisiana into two divisions: the Orleans Territory and the Louisiana District. Orleans was the more heavily populated lower Mississippi region. Its capital was New Orleans, and it was basically the modern-day state of Louisiana. The Louisiana District was the large upper segment of the region and contained St. Louis. Only Orleans was guaranteed eventual statehood.

Neither region was to be allowed much self-government. If, under France and then Spain, the Louisiana Purchase region had been a colony ruled with a firm hand from afar, it still was. Jefferson and Congress treated their new domain exactly as a U.S. colony, merely substituting an American hand for a Spanish one. According to Attorney General Levi Lincoln, the president and Congress had almost unlimited power in both the Orleans and Louisiana Territories. Consequently, the federal government's authority was again broadened and strengthened by the Louisiana Purchase.

GOVERNING LOUISIANA

It was the president who appointed the Orleans Territory's chief official, the governor, who served for three years. The governor, in turn, appointed many of the other territorial officials, particularly militia officers, of whom he was the commander in chief. He also enforced all laws, whether federal or territorial.

Legislation that affected only Orleans was proposed and voted on by a council that included the governor and thirteen others. Once more, it was the president who appointed the council members, each of whom served a one-year term. This scheme was modified in late 1804 when Congress created a territorial assembly, elected by Orleans residents. The original council was kept, but now laws and regulations had to pass both bodies before going to the governor, who could veto any legislation. The U.S. Congress periodically reviewed these laws and could remove any of them it so desired. The assembly and council also elected a delegate who represented Orleans in Congress.

The Louisiana District was originally placed under the governor of the Indiana Territory. However, in July 1805 Congress removed the district from Indiana, renamed it the Louisiana Territory, made St. Louis its capital, and gave it its own governor, another three-year presidential appointee. Unlike in Orleans, the Louisiana Territory governor had absolute authority within the region, there being no council or assembly. Thus, he not only executed laws but decreed them. He was accountable to both the president and Congress.

LIMITED RIGHTS

In both the Orleans and Louisiana Territories, the historian Thomas Perkins Abernethy adds,

LOUISIANIANS DEMAND THEIR RIGHTS

The non-American residents of Louisiana soon discovered that they were not to receive instant U.S. citizenship nor be allowed to govern themselves, for the American government did not think the French and Spanish inhabitants ready for citizenship, let alone self-rule. In 1804, hoping to sway Congress into granting these rights, Pierre Derbigney sent to Washington, D.C., the following grievance, reprinted in The Boisterous Sea of Liberty.

"It was early understood that we were to be American citizens; this satisfied our wishes. . . . Even the evils of a military . . . authority were acquiesced in [accepted], because it indicated an eagerness to complete the transfer, and place beyond the reach of accident the union we mutually desired. . . .

We pray leave to examine the law for erecting [governing] Louisiana. . . . A Governor is to be placed over us, whom we have not chosen, whom we do not even know. . . .

The Governor is invested with [given] all executive, and almost unlimited legislative power, for the law declares that 'by and with the advice . . . of the legislative body he may change, modify and repeal the laws.' . . . But . . . this council, selected by the President or Governor, . . . [is] dependent on him for their appointment and continuance in office. . . . the true legislative power is vested in the Governor. . . .

Taxation without representation, an obligation to obey the laws, without any voice in their formation . . . formed . . . very prominent articles in the list of grievances complained of by the United States at the commencement of their glorious contest for freedom. . . . Are truths . . . so well founded . . . inapplicable [unsuited] only for us?"

the American judicial system was introduced, English became the official language, and the Creoles [the French and Spanish inhabitants] were required to prove their land titles and to pay taxes—things that they had never been made to do under the Spanish regime.[40]

The land title and tax requirements brought complaints from the Creoles, who felt that their established rights were being violated. They also complained that, except for the Orleans assembly, they had no voice in either the national or the territorial governments. Indeed, the American citizenship that was supposedly theirs according to the Louisiana Purchase Treaty had not been, nor was being, offered to them.

In fact, neither the Jefferson administration nor the majority of Congress had any immediate intention of making the Creoles U.S. citizens. Few in the federal government believed that these former Spanish subjects were capable of understanding self-government, having lived their lives under the autocratic rule of Spain. Alexander DeConde observes,

Despite Thomas Jefferson's frequently expressed commitment to democratic principles, he . . . believed that Louisiana should not enter the Union on

ST. LOUIS

In his Views of Louisiana, *Henry Marie Brackenridge provides the following 1811 description of St. Louis, which would have been much the same seven years before when Lewis and Clark set out on their journey up the Missouri.*

"[St. Louis] was formerly called Pain Court, from the privations [hardships] of the first settlers. . . . In a disjointed and scattered manner it extends along the river a mile and a half, and we form the idea of a large and elegant town. Two or three large costly buildings . . . contribute in producing this effect. . . .

[Inland] there is a line of works . . . , erected for defense against the Indians, consisting of several circular towers, . . . a small stockaded fort, and a stone breast work [wall]. These are . . . entirely unoccupied . . . , excepting the fort, in one of the buildings of which, the [law] courts are held, while another is used as a prison. . . .

St. Louis contains . . . 1,400 inhabitants. . . . Every house is crowded, rents are high, and it is difficult to obtain . . . [lodging] on any terms. . . . There is a printing office, and twelve . . . stores. . . . The outfits [clothing] for different trading establishments, on the Mississippi or Missouri, are made here. . . . The settlers in the vicinity on both sides of the river, repair [come] to this place as the best market for their produce, and to supply themselves with such articles as they may need. . . .

St. Louis . . . was always a place of more refinement and fashion [than surrounding villages], it is the residence of many genteel [cultured] families, both French and American. . . . There is a French school and an English one."

the basis of equality with existing units, at least not at once. He presumed that the people of . . . Louisiana, having lived under despotic [oppressive] rule, were not ready to govern themselves. He maintained that the Creoles . . . would not make good citizens until they learned the meaning of democracy. He viewed Louisiana as a possession not immediately acceptable within the Union.[41]

THE BORDERS OF LOUISIANA

Although the territorial governments of Orleans and Louisiana had authority throughout both regions, in reality their influence was confined to the settlements along the Mississippi. The remainder of the territories were inhabited mostly by Native Americans, who were unaware that they had ever been under the rule of Spain or that they were now part of the United States.

Just how far American authority reached even in theory was not clear, for neither France nor Spain had ever established fixed borders for the Louisiana colony, except along the Mississippi River. All that U.S. officials knew was that the region they had bought stretched from the yet undiscovered source of the Mississippi in the north to the Red River in the south, with a jag along the Mississippi to the Gulf of Mexico. The purchased land ended in the west somewhere among the Rocky Mountains. But where exactly American land stopped and British territory in the north and Spanish in the east, southwest, and west started was anyone's guess.

DESIRING FLORIDA

These uncertain borders provided Jefferson with an opportunity to renew his quest for western Florida, even though both France and Spain denied that it was a part of the purchase. Nonetheless, at the urging of Robert Livingston, the Jefferson administration claimed Florida as far east as the Perdido River. Livingston advised that old French maps showed this river as the southeastern border of Louisiana. This strip of land was very desirable because it contained the mouths of several rivers running from U.S. territory to the Gulf of Mexico as well as Mobile Bay, which would make an excellent naval port.

The Spanish would not even discuss giving up any part of Florida. They pointed out that the region Jefferson wanted had not been given to them by France with the rest of Louisiana, it had been ceded by the British in the 1783 Treaty of Paris. In no way, regardless of any old maps, could western Florida be considered part of the land bought by the United States.

Jefferson did not admit defeat. If Spain would not give up western Florida, would they sell it? Again the answer was no.

Jefferson's response was to threaten Spain with an American invasion and capture of all of Florida.

A BID FOR TEXAS

While this unfriendly wrangling over Florida continued, Jefferson's attention turned west. While speaking with French officials at New Orleans, William Claiborne had been told that France had once claimed all the land west to the Rio Grande. Acting on this information, Jefferson felt confident in claiming all of Texas, which lay between the Red River and the Rio Grande.

Texas, however, was not as important to Jefferson as western Florida, or indeed all of Florida. Thus, he was willing to use Texas as a bargaining chip. DeConde describes the administration's strategy:

> In February [1804] the cabinet backed the president by approving three alternative territorial offers to Spain. For recognition of the Perdido boundary the United States would give up its claim to Texas. For a line farther east on the Apalachicola River it would close a broad belt of territory on the western frontier [between the U.S. and Spanish land] to white settlers for a . . . number of years. For both the Floridas it would supplement these concessions with "one million dollars."[42]

JEFFERSON BACKS DOWN

Jefferson, through James Monroe, sought French help in persuading the Spanish to give over some of the contested land. However, Napoléon refused to take America's side. In early 1805 Talleyrand-Périgord wrote to Jefferson that Napoléon, who was now emperor, was shocked by America's use of the Louisiana Purchase Treaty to threaten Spanish holdings in North America. France then signed a treaty with Spain, ensuring the safety of the latter's territory.

Meanwhile, the Spanish response had been to put troops along the boundaries of both Florida and Texas to repel any invasion by the United States. By the summer of 1805, however, Jefferson had decided that acquiring even western Florida was not worth a war with both Spain and France. Still tensions persisted along the various American-Spanish borders, even though the immediate crisis passed.

RAIDERS AND CONSPIRATORS

The U.S. clash with Spain over Florida and Texas opened a door for a number of opportunists. In June 1804 a pair of what were known as frontier roughnecks, Nathan and Samuel Kemper, pretended to lead a revolt of Americans living in Spanish Florida. In reality, the two men were only interested in raiding and plundering and finally fled with their loot across the U.S. border.

Much more ambitious was the Burr conspiracy, organized by Aaron Burr and General James Wilkinson. Burr had been vice president during Jefferson's first term in office. He had arrived in New Orleans in 1804, having fled New Jersey and a warrant for his arrest for recently killing his political rival, Alexander Hamilton, in a duel.

Wilkinson was governor of the Louisiana Territory and had been involved for

Aaron Burr was charged with treason for his alleged attempt to take over Mexico and part of Louisiana.

most of his life in political intrigue. Beginning in the late 1780s, Spain paid him to urge Kentuckians to secede from the Union. At the same time, Wilkinson was working his way up the chain of command in the U.S. Army, becoming its commanding general in 1797.

THE BURR CONSPIRACY

In 1805 Burr and Wilkinson drew up plans to invade Mexico and take over all or part of that Spanish colony. Addition-

ally, the two—or perhaps Burr alone—may have planned to capture part of the Louisiana Territory and, combining this region with Mexican land, form an empire modeled on Napoléonic France, with Burr as emperor. Whether the Burr conspiracy included this second objective remains a mystery to this day.

In 1806 Wilkinson lost his taste for the conspiracy and betrayed Burr and their plans to federal officials. The general felt that Burr had talked too freely and that word of their venture was now known in Washington, D.C. Burr was ordered arrested and was captured trying to flee to Spanish territory.

Jefferson had Burr tried for treason because of the alleged plan to take over American land. Burr denied that he had ever schemed against the United States, and indeed, the federal government could produce no evidence of such a plot. Consequently, he was acquitted of treason charges. Wilkinson was also cleared of any wrongdoing in a series of court-martials, although he was removed as governor of the Louisiana Territory.

THE CORPS OF DISCOVERY

Border disputes, threats of war, and conspiracies were by no means all that interested Thomas Jefferson about the Louisiana Purchase. Above all else, he wanted to know more about the land, the animals and plants, and the people living there. Accordingly, he sponsored a number of expeditions to explore the region.

The first of these endeavors was the Lewis and Clark expedition, also known as the Corps of Discovery. Planned by Jefferson even before he knew that France was willing to sell Louisiana, the expedition was to look for a water route to the Pacific coast. Additionally, the explorers were to collect as much information about the region and its inhabitants as they could.

Heading the Corps of Discovery were Captain Meriwether Lewis and Lieutenant William Clark, both of Virginia and both officers in the U.S. Army. Thirty-year-old Lewis was an expert hunter with much experience exploring various eastern wilderness areas. He had been Jefferson's private secretary and the president handpicked the young captain for command. Upon his appointment as one of the expedition leaders, Lewis went to Philadelphia to study botany, zoology, and navigation.

Clark was thirty-three and was quite experienced in dealing with Indians. He had fought in a number of campaigns against Native Americans, but he had also learned much about various Indian cultures, coming to respect the people and their customs. Additionally, he was the map maker and expedition artist and would produce a host of very detailed maps as well as excellent paintings of Louisiana wildlife.

Meriwether Lewis (left) and William Clark (right) were chosen to lead the expedition that would investigate the area acquired through the Louisiana Purchase.

This painting depicts the Lewis and Clark expedition stopping along the bluffs of the Missouri River to record their observations.

UP THE MISSOURI

The rest of the Corps of Discovery were some forty healthy young men, among whom were meteorologists, botanists, zoologists, gunsmiths, carpenters, and boat operators. All were used to outdoor living. In a camp near St. Louis during the winter of 1803–1804, Lewis and Clark drilled these men in military matters. They also collected supplies and equipment. Then, on May 14, 1804, the entire expedition set sail up the Missouri.

Over the next year and a half, the party traveled the length of the Missouri, crossed the Rockies and the Continental Divide, and canoed down the Clearwater, Snake, and Columbia Rivers to the Pacific Ocean, which they reached on November 15, 1805. The return trip took almost another year, with the corps arriving back at St. Louis on September 23, 1806.

A WEALTH OF INFORMATION

Lewis, Clark, and company finally put an end to the myth of a water passage to the west coast. More importantly, they brought back maps marked accurately with latitude and longitude. Furthermore, in the form of diaries and journals, they provided descriptions of hundreds of birds, fish, animals, plants, and trees. The following entry from Lewis's journal, dated May 3, 1805, is typical of the information to be found in the expedition's records:

> Near the entrance of the river [where it entered the Missouri] . . . , we saw a unusual number of Porcupines from which we determined to call the river after that anamal [sic]. . . .

> I walked out a little distance and met with 2 porcupines which were feeding on the young willow which grow in great abundance on all the sandbars;

this animal is exceedingly clumsy and not very watchfull [sic] . . . [I] found the nest of a wild goose among some driftwood in the river. . . . This is the only nest we have met with on driftwood, the usual position is the top of a broken tree, . . . from 15 to 20 feet or upwards high.[43]

The party also collected many living and dead animal and plant samples. Among the live specimens that eventually arrived in Washington, D.C., was a prairie dog. The Corps of Discovery also established friendly relations with dozens of Native American tribes, many of whom wanted trade with the United States. As Dale van Every writes, "As a physical and

Sacagawea (right) proved to be a valuable asset to the Lewis and Clark expedition, helping the group to establish friendly relations with various Indian tribes.

moral achievement the undertaking had been a monumental success. . . . As practitioners of the art of exploration they were truly professionals."[44]

THE GRAND EXCURSION

Even as the Corps of Discovery was starting up the Missouri, Jefferson was deep in plans for a similar enterprise to probe the length of the Red River. Known as the Grand Excursion, or the Freeman and Custis expedition, this venture was led by Thomas Freeman, a young Irish American surveyor and amateur astronomer, and Peter Custis, an American-trained naturalist.

The Grand Excursion began its ascent of the Red River on April 28, 1806, but was cut short when, three months later, it ran into a party of 150 Spanish soldiers. The Spaniards insisted that the Americans were trespassing on Spanish land and forced them to turn around and return home.

The results of the Grand Excursion were disappointing in light of the information brought back by Lewis and Clark. But even in a mere three months, Freeman was able to compile enough data to compose an excellent map of the first six hundred miles of the Red River. And as historian Dan L. Flores notes, Custis provided "a valuable and intriguing ecological investigation of the Red River valley's natural history."[45]

ZEBULON PIKE

As the Grand Excursion came to its untimely end, a young army lieutenant, Zebulon Montgomery Pike, was setting out on July 15, 1806, from St. Louis. On orders from General James Wilkinson, Pike and his small party of twenty-three soldiers were to explore west along the Arkansas River.

In November the soldiers reached the Rocky Mountains just as winter was setting in. Neither Pike nor his men had the proper clothing for the freezing winds and deep snow. Despite these conditions, Pike attempted to climb the peak that now bears his name. Failing to even reach the mountain, he returned to his base camp after thirty-six hours without food.

The hardships continued as Pike led his men south through the mountains and into New Mexico. Several of his party were permanently disabled by frostbite before they reached the Spanish settlement of Sante Fe, where they were arrested. Their presence confirmed Spain's worst fear: that Americans would soon find their way from Louisiana to the Spanish southwest. The Pike party was eventually escorted back to American territory in July 1807.

TRADERS AND MOUNTAIN MEN

Pike's report on Sante Fe stressed the military weakness of the Spanish garrison and the possibilities of trade with New Mexico. This account would spark much interest in American merchants and send them in increasingly larger numbers across the Orleans and Louisiana Territories and into New Mexico.

A HARD TREK

Exploring the Louisiana Territory was no easy task, as Zebulon Pike and his party found out when caught in a snowstorm in the mountains of Colorado during January 1807. This excerpt is from an entry in Zebulon Pike's Arkansas Journal.

"The doctor and myself [Pike] proceeded on ahead in hopes to kill something, as we were again without victuals [food]. About one o'clock it commenced snowing very hard. We retreated to a small copse [grove] of pine where we constructed a camp.... We lay down and strove to dissipate [dismiss] the idea of hunger and our misery by the thoughts of our far distant homes and relatives....

We sallied out in the morning.... I determined to attempt the traverse [crossing] of the mountain, in which we persevered, until the snow became so deep, it was impossible to proceed; when I again turned my face [turned back] to the plain and for the first time in the voyage found myself discouraged; and the first time I heard a man express himself in a seditious [mutinous] manner; he exclaimed, 'that it was more than human nature could bear, to march three days without sustenance [food], through snows three feet deep, and carry burthens only fit for horses.' ...

We dragged our weary and emaciated [starved] limbs along, until about 10 o'clock. The doctor and myself who were in advance discovered some buffalo on the plain.... We went in pursuit of the buffalo....

The doctor who was then less reduced than myself, ran and ... shot one down. . . . We then proceeded to butcher the one we had shot."

Many difficulties and hardships plagued the expedition led by Zebulon Pike.

Other traders were also setting out to retrace the footsteps of Lewis and Clark. They sought trade with the Indians of the region, being particularly interested in furs. As van Every writes, "If furnished the initial capital for boats, equipment, and trade goods hundreds of men were eager to go."[46]

Some of these early trading ventures ended in disaster, their members killed by Native Americans such as the Blackfeet, who resented these invaders. The ones who survived began to trap singly rather than as members of a company. These men would roam the entire Louisiana Territory, coming to know its land and its native peoples. Eventually known as mountain men, they would often adopt the dress and lifestyles of the Indians, who would also provide them with wives.

FLORIDA AND LOUISIANA

Even as trappers moved into the western reaches of the Louisiana Territory, crisis once more came to western Florida. In the summer of 1810, American settlers in the Spanish colony successfully revolted and declared their independence from Spain. They immediately petitioned James Madison, who had succeeded Jefferson as president the previous year, to be added to the United States. Madison ordered Governor Claiborne to take possession of the region and make it part of the Orleans Territory. Although Madison expected Claiborne to occupy the land as far east as the Perdido River, the governor and his troops only went as far as the Pearl River.

Spain protested the seizure of this land, as did their new ally, England. England had come to Spain's aid after Napoléon had placed his brother Joseph on the Spanish throne two years before. Madison ignored these protests, replying that the United States was merely claiming what rightfully belonged to it under the Louisiana Purchase Treaty.

Two years later, on April 30, the Pearl River became the easternmost border of the newly created state of Louisiana, formerly the Orleans Territory. The state, admitted exactly nine years after the signing of the purchase treaty, was still sparsely settled, but it had gained at least thirty thousand people in the previous decade, bringing its population to eighty thousand. More than half of the state's residents were already American citizens. To avoid confusion with the new state, the Louisiana Territory was renamed the Missouri Territory.

THE WAR OF 1812

On June 18, only six weeks after Louisiana became a state, President Madison declared war on Great Britain. The War of 1812 had a number of causes, and some of them were tied to the country's western territory. Western Americans were angry because the English, from Canada, were providing guns and supplies to the Shawnee Indians and encouraging them to attack American citizens. The English hoped to drive U.S. trappers out of the fur trade, which England longed to monopolize. Additionally, American supporters of the war saw it as an opportunity to force Spain into battle on the English side and thus justify an invasion of the remainder of Florida.

Although the United States had some success in the war, particularly at sea and in fighting on Lakes Erie and Ontario, it also had some spectacular defeats, such as the capture of Washington, D.C., and the burning of the public buildings there. In general, however, the war ground on without a clear victory for either side for over two years. Weary of the whole mess, the United States and Great Britain signed a peace treaty on December 24, 1814, at Ghent, Belgium.

THE BATTLE OF NEW ORLEANS

Although the war had ended at the conference table in Belgium, it was far from over in Louisiana, where news of the peace would not reach until weeks after the signing of the treaty and where the British were preparing to launch an attack on New Orleans.

On January 8, 1815, General Sir Edward Pakenham led some seventy-five hundred seasoned British troops against some six thousand American militia and volunteers commanded by General Andrew Jackson. Pakenham was confident that he could overrun the less-experienced Americans and take New Orleans.

Jackson, however, had built himself and his forces a barricade made of cotton bales, which he had thrown across a narrow neck of land, with water on one side and a swamp on the other. From openings left in the bales, the defenders poured a

The United States scored a stunning victory over the British in the Battle of New Orleans even though the peace treaty ending the War of 1812 had been signed weeks earlier.

THE BATTLE OF NEW ORLEANS

James Roberts was one of several hundred black slaves recruited by Andrew Jackson, who promised them freedom if they would help fight the British at New Orleans. Jackson did not keep his promise, but Roberts did win his freedom years later and left this firsthand account of the battle in The Narrative of James Roberts.

"We marched forward until we came in sight of the British army, and the first view of it was very impressive indeed. The British soldiers wore large, brilliant steel breast-plates, steel caps and steel covers on their arms. . . .

[British commander] Packenham drew up his army along the water side, and remained there two days. . . . A colored soldier . . . gave Jackson the . . . idea about the *cotton-bag fort*. . . . We engaged in making it. . . . The cotton-bags were so placed as to leave. . . . holes for three muskets to point through each. . . .

On the third day, . . . the British fired. They fired three rounds, and [with] the fourth we opened [fire] on them. . . . They began to throw [artillery] shells into our fort, and had they continued . . ., there is no doubt that victory would have been easy to them. But Packenham, . . . impatient to carry everything by main force, . . . rushed [his troops] forward . . . ; and, as they came, we felled them like grass before the scythe [cutting tool]. . . . [They] lay like scattered hail upon the ground. Packenham seeing this, and observing the rapid loss of his men, marched them single file up to our fort. He himself mounted the wall. . . . Instead of ordering the bags to be pushed inside next to us, he ordered them to be pulled outside, which entangled his men, . . . and we slew them by the scores."

Andrew Jackson led the United States to victory in the Battle of New Orleans.

murderous fire into the attacking British, packed tight by the narrow approach to the American stronghold. In less than half an hour, the Battle of New Orleans was over, with some two thousand English casualties, Pakenham being one of the dead.

FLORIDA ONCE MORE

In addition to saving New Orleans from a temporary, or perhaps even permanent, British occupation, western American forces also captured the remaining segment of western Florida between the Pearl and Perdido Rivers. Three years after the Battle of New Orleans, Andrew Jackson led troops into the remainder of Florida and took it over, even though he had no official permission from Washington, D.C., to do so. Jackson claimed that Native American raiders were operating out of the Spanish colony, and U.S. possession of the territory was the only way to stop them.

Secretary of State John Quincy Adams began immediate negotiations with Spain to buy Florida as well as to establish the boundary line between the Louisiana Purchase region and Spanish North America. Adams believed Spain was ready to settle these matters since that nation was drained financially and militarily by the revolt of most of its South American colonies.

FINAL BORDERS

At the same time that Adams was dealing with the Spanish, other American diplo-

Secretary of State John Quincy Adams successfully negotiated the purchase of Florida from Spain.

mats were holding talks in London about the border between the western United States and Canada. On October 20, 1818, the U.S. and English representatives signed a convention that fixed the northern boundary of the Missouri Territory as the forty-ninth degree of latitude running west from the Lake of the Woods to the Rocky Mountains.

Four months later, on February 22, 1819, the Adams-Onís Treaty recognized America's possession of Florida in exchange for assuming $5 million in claims against Spain by U.S. citizens. In addition, according to Marshall Sprague,

It [the treaty] made a permanent boundary for . . . [the Louisiana Purchase territory] . . . , using the Sabine River north from the Gulf of Mexico, the Red River west to the 100th meridian, and the Arkansas [River] to its source. From the source of the Arkansas, the Louisiana line ran due north to the 42d parallel, and then due west to the Continental Divide—in present Wyoming.[47]

The United States had now fixed the shape and extent of the Louisiana Purchase. But it had yet to grow into the region. That process would take the remainder of the nineteenth century as settlers filled up the margin of the Mississippi River and then pushed westward into the Great Plains.

Growth and Settlement

The final development of the Louisiana Purchase was neither quick nor easy. It saw both triumph and injustice. In the end, however, the wild land that Jefferson bought was gone, replaced by farms and cities.

SETTLERS AND SLAVES

While the United States was stabilizing the borders of the Louisiana Purchase, it was also building a series of army forts along the Arkansas and Missouri Rivers. These posts were to offer protection to settlers in the region. And settlers were indeed coming into the Missouri Territory. In part, they were seeking relief from an economic depression that had gripped the nation in the wake of the War of 1812. However, they also sought the pioneer's old dream of new opportunities and new beginnings.

The promise of new opportunities and adventure led to the rapid settlement of Missouri.

The settlement of Missouri went rapidly, and by 1821 it became the second state to be carved from the Louisiana Purchase. Missouri presented the country with a problem: how to handle the issue of slavery in the West. At the time, there were eleven slave and eleven free states. Missouri, which sought to be a slave state, would shatter that balance.

There were those who wished to keep slavery out of the whole territory entirely, and others who were just as determined to make slavery a part of the West. An attempt in Congress to abolish slavery in Missouri failed. To keep the number of free and slave states even, antislavery Maine was admitted at the same time as Missouri. Slavery was then banned north of a line that extended from Missouri's southern border through the rest of the western territory. This arrangement, which balanced the interests of the two factions, was known as the Missouri Compromise.

THE GREAT AMERICAN DESERT

Except for traders and trappers such as the mountain men, few Americans were to be found west of Missouri. This area was the Great Plains, which dominated the center of the Louisiana Purchase. Most Americans believed the region to be uninhabitable, despite the presence of a quarter million Plains Indians. One explorer of the region, Stephen Long, wrote of his 1820 trek through the expanse:

We have little apprehension [fear] of giving too unfavorable an account of

this portion of the country. . . . The want of timber, of navigable streams, and of water . . . render it an unfit residence for any but a nomade [sic] population. . . . It is almost totally unfit for cultivation.[48]

The Plains became known as the Great American Desert. Yet despite its glorious name, most Americans refused to live there. They did not, however, avoid it, for part of the Oregon Trail passed through the Great Plains. Beginning with the first party in 1842, thousands of migrants passed along this trail, which stretched from Independence, Missouri, to the Willamette Valley in Oregon. Portions of the trail were also used by those traveling to California.

THE PLAINS INDIANS

The line of forts along the Arkansas and Missouri Rivers was extended farther west along the Oregon Trail. The wagon trains of the Oregon pioneers brought Americans in contact with the Plains Indians, and although most of these contacts were peaceful, not all were. The forts and the presence of the U.S. Army served to protect the travelers.

Whereas in the past Native American villages could be found along the rivers, the horse had brought a new freedom to the nomadic hunters. Indeed, new nomads were on the scene. Groups such as the Cheyenne and the Dakota, or Sioux, who had not been plains dwellers but rather hunters and fishers located in Minnesota,

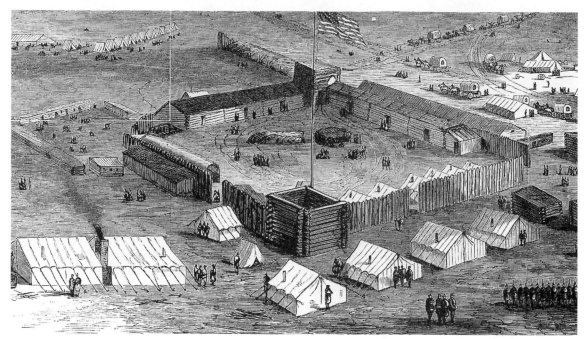

U.S. Army forts were built along the Great Plains as an ever-increasing number of settlers headed west.

had moved out onto the Great Plains during the end of the eighteenth century. Here, they had created a wild, colorful, and sometimes violent culture.

The first real eastern settlers of the Great Plains were themselves Native Americans. Even before the Louisiana Purchase, the federal government had encouraged eastern Indians to migrate west in the hopes that this move would eventually eliminate the competition between settlers and Indians. After the purchase, the United States began forcing Native Americans to move into the Indian Territory, which is now present-day Oklahoma. One of the most infamous cases of this policy was the removal of the Cherokee from Georgia in 1838. Much of their forced march west to the Indian Territory

was during winter, leading to the death of a quarter of their number.

BLEEDING KANSAS

By the early 1850s, despite the reputation of the Great Plains, white settlers were edging into the Kansas and Nebraska Territories. To lure more people into these regions, Senator Stephen A. Douglas proposed a bill in 1854 that would eliminate the Missouri Compromise and leave the determination of whether a western territory should be slave or free up to the territorial legislature.

Historian Steven E. Siry describes the tragic results of Douglas's bill: "As proslavery and antislavery groups competed for control in the area, violence . . . escalated until the territory became known as 'Bleeding Kansas.'"[49] In the end, the antislavery forces won out, and Kansas entered the Union in 1861, on the eve of the Civil War, as a free state.

THE HOMESTEAD ACT

Even while the Civil War raged, Congress looked for ways to encourage more settlement of the Great Plains. In 1862, it passed the Homestead Act, which offered 160 acres of land for a ten-dollar fee to anyone who promised to live on and work the land for at least five years. Eventually over four hundred thousand families would gain land on the Great Plains through this act.

Because water was almost always in short supply and because irrigation systems did not yet exist in the Great Plains farming communities, a farm had to be much larger than 160 acres to be self-supporting. A second congressional bill, the Timber Act, offered an additional 160 acres to any landowner who would agree to plant trees on a quarter of his property within a four-year span.

Many found the wide-open, treeless vistas of the Great Plains depressing, but others adjusted well. They built their homes out of sod bricks and burned corncobs instead of wood. They also found that the soil made for rich farmland, and

The debate over slavery in Kansas often led to violent confrontations between proslavery and antislavery factions.

these plains farms increased U.S. food production enormously. Western Minnesota and eastern North Dakota in particular proved to produce some of the highest yields of wheat and corn in the world.

THE INDIAN WARS

Despite the thousands who traveled the Oregon Trail, it was not until the settlers came to the Great Plains that the Native Americans of the region realized that their very way of life was threatened. The huge herds of buffalo, upon which the Plains Indians depended, were virtually wiped out in the twenty years after the Civil War by hunters for the railroads. The railroads did further damage by pushing through tribal lands, supposedly guaranteed by treaty, and bringing even more settlers with them.

Indian resistance from the time of the Civil War through the 1890s was often violent. A gold strike in the Black Hills of the Dakota Territory brought swarms of miners. The Dakota tribes, which held these mountains to be sacred, went to war. Along with the Cheyenne, the Dakota handed the U.S. Army a smashing defeat on June 25, 1876, when the warring tribes killed George Armstrong Custer and six hundred of his command at the Little Bighorn, known to the Indians as Greasy Grass. In the end, the final

Settlement of the Great Plains and the construction of railroads led to the near extinction of the buffalo.

Custer's Last Stand was one of the many battles fought in the ongoing wars between the United States and the Plains Indians.

victory went to the army, which had the numbers and the weapons.

THE END OF THE TERRITORY

By the start of the twentieth century, the Great Plains and the rest of old Louisiana were tamed, their beginnings nothing more than a memory. In 1904, to honor that memory, the St. Louis Exposition was held to commemorate the hundredth anniversary of the Louisiana Purchase.

Three years after the exposition, Oklahoma was admitted as a state, and the last vestige of the old, unincorporated territory was gone. The United States had bought a wilderness and, for better or worse, altered it and made it a part of itself. Marshall Sprague writes,

> It took time, trial and error, science and invention, for the settlers to transform La Salle's wilderness into today's domesticated thirteen states [made from the Louisiana Purchase]—all of the nineteenth century. . . . Through those years, the magnificent empire that Napoleon surrendered for fifteen million . . . dollars has poured forth its bounty from generation to generation. And yet it is a young empire still, . . . its promise as infinite as when Jefferson yearned to possess it for freedom's sake.[50]

Notes

Introduction: The New Territory

1. Alexander DeConde, *This Affair of Louisiana*. New York: Scribner's, 1976, p. 209.

2. Quoted in Fred L. Israel, ed., *Major Presidential Decisions*. New York: Chelsea House, 1980, p. 148.

3. Marshall Sprague, *So Vast So Beautiful a Land: Louisiana and the Purchase*. Boston: Little, Brown, 1974, p. xvii.

4. Sprague, *So Vast So Beautiful a Land*, p. xix.

Chapter 1: The Making of Louisiana

5. Michael Coe, Dean Snow, and Elizabeth Benson, *Atlas of Ancient America*. New York: Facts On File, 1986, pp. 57–58.

6. Sprague, *So Vast So Beautiful a Land*, p. 8.

7. David Ewing Duncan, *Hernando de Soto: A Savage Conquest in the Americas*. New York: Crown, 1995, p. xix.

8. Quoted in Sprague, *So Vast So Beautiful a Land*, p. 34.

9. DeConde, *This Affair of Louisiana*, p. 14.

10. James K. Hosmer, *The History of the Louisiana Purchase*. New York: D. Appleton, 1902, p. 13.

11. James Q. Howard, *History of the Louisiana Purchase*. Chicago: Callaghan, 1902, p. 31.

12. E. Wilson Lyon, *Louisiana in French Diplomacy: 1759–1804*. Norman: University of Oklahoma Press, 1934, p. 33.

Chapter 2: Uneasy Relations

13. DeConde, *This Affair of Louisiana*, p. 49.

14. Quoted in DeConde, *This Affair of Louisiana*, p. 41.

15. Quoted in Sprague, *So Vast So Beautiful a Land*, p. 266.

16. DeConde, *This Affair of Louisiana*, p. 45.

17. Sprague, *So Vast So Beautiful a Land*, p. 266.

18. Hosmer, *The History of the Louisiana Purchase*, p. 30.

19. Lyon, *Louisiana in French Diplomacy*, p. 88.

20. Quoted in Lyon, *Louisiana in French Diplomacy*, p. 108.

21. DeConde, *This Affair of Louisiana*, p. 95.

Chapter 3: The Louisiana Crisis

22. Quoted in DeConde, *This Affair of Louisiana*, p. 111.

23. Sprague, *So Vast So Beautiful a Land*, p. 273.

24. DeConde, *This Affair of Louisiana*, p. 97.

25. Quoted in Lyon, *Louisiana in French Diplomacy*, p. 120.

26. Quoted in Israel, *Major Presidential Decisions*, p. 46.

27. Quoted in DeConde, *This Affair of Louisiana*, p. 124.

28. Quoted in Israel, *Major Presidential Decisions*, p. 130.

29. Lyon, *Louisiana in French Diplomacy*, p. 202.

30. Quoted in DeConde, *This Affair of Louisiana*, p. 157.

Chapter 4: Taking Possession

31. Quoted in DeConde, *This Affair of Louisiana*, p. 178.

32. Quoted in Hosmer, *The History of the Louisiana Purchase*, p. 218.

33. Quoted in DeConde, *This Affair of Louisiana*, p. 184.

34. Quoted in Sprague, *So Vast So Beautiful a Land*, pp. 314–15.

35. Hosmer, *The History of the Louisiana Purchase*, pp. 151–52.

36. Quoted in Gerhard Casper, *Separating Power: Essays on the Founding Period*. Cambridge, MA: Harvard University Press, 1997, p. 129.

37. Casper, *Separating Power*, p. 129.

38. DeConde, *This Affair of Louisiana*, p. 202.

39. Quoted in Israel, *Major Presidential Decisions*, p. 189.

Chapter 5: Exploration, Conspiracy, and War

40. Thomas Perkins Abernethy, *The Burr Conspiracy*. New York: Oxford University Press, 1954, pp. 16–17.

41. DeConde, *This Affair of Louisiana*, pp. 210–11.

42. DeConde, *This Affair of Louisiana*, p. 217.

43. Meriwether Lewis and William Clark, *The Journals of Lewis and Clark*, ed. Frank Bergon. New York: Penguin Books, 1989, p. 114.

44. Dale Van Every, *The Final Challenge: The American Frontier, 1804–1845*. New York: Morrow, 1964, p. 68.

45. Dan L. Flores, ed., *Jefferson and Southwestern Exploration: The Freeman and Custis Accounts of the Red River Expedition of 1806*. Norman: University of Oklahoma Press, 1984, p. 297.

46. Van Every, *The Final Challenge*, p. 93.

47. Sprague, *So Vast So Beautiful a Land*, pp. 327–28.

Conclusion: Growth and Settlement

48. Quoted in Van Every, *The Final Challenge*, pp. 163–64.

49. Quoted in John E. Findling and Frank W. Thackeray, eds., *Events That Changed America in the Nineteenth Century*. Westport, CT: Greenwood, 1997, p. 10.

50. Sprague, *So Vast So Beautiful a Land*, p. 328.

For Further Reading

Books

Gary L. Blackwood, *Life on the Oregon Trail.* San Diego: Lucent Books, 1999. Filled with illustrations and eyewitness accounts, this study looks at what it was like to cross the Great Plains on the way to Oregon.

Bob Carroll, *Napoléon Bonaparte.* San Diego: Lucent Books, 1994. A readable biography of the life of the ruler of France who sold Louisiana to America. Extensive quotations from the period and later, a time line of Napoléon's life, and a reading list add to the value of the text.

Robert Carson, *Hernando de Soto.* Chicago: Childrens, 1999. Filled with illustrations, some in color, maps, and a reading list, this solid biography covers the life of this early Spanish explorer and conqueror, particularly his trek to the Mississippi and beyond.

Jim Collins, *Mountain Men.* New York: Franklin Watts, 1996. A series of biographical sketches of famous trappers and frontiersmen, including Jim Bridger and Kit Carson, which detail their lives and outlooks. The text is supplemented by many illustrations and a bibliography.

Tony Coulter, *La Salle and the Explorers of the Mississippi.* New York: Chelsea House, 1991. A good illustrated survey of both Spanish and French exploration of the Mississippi River.

Eleanor J. Hall, *The Lewis and Clark Expedition.* San Diego: Lucent Books, 1996. Describes the travels and discoveries of the first American explorers of Louisiana. Included also are many illustrations, a time line, and a reading list.

Harry Henderson, *The Age of Napoleon.* San Diego: Lucent Books, 1999. A good short history of Napoléonic France, describing its wars and shifting political alliances. The text is supported by illustrations, a chronology, and a bibliography.

Virginia Branard Kunz, *The French in America.* Minneapolis: Lerner, 1990. A good survey of France's role in American history from the sixteenth century on.

Don Nardo, *Thomas Jefferson.* San Diego: Lucent Books, 1993. Details the life and achievements of the president who bought Louisiana. The text is enhanced by illustrations and the words of the man and his contemporaries.

———, *The War of 1812.* San Diego: Lucent Books, 2000. Supported by reports of participants, maps, and illustrations, this account describes the course of the war, including the Battle of New Orleans. Additional material includes a time line and reading list.

Wendi C. Old, *James Monroe.* Springfield, NJ: Enslow, 1998. Illustrations, maps, and a bibliography strengthen this account of the life and accomplishments of one of the negotiators of the Louisiana Purchase Treaty.

Earle Rice Jr., *Life Among the Great Plains Indians.* San Diego: Lucent Books, 1998. This account combines eyewitness sketches with illustrations and photographs to bring to life the way the Plains Indians lived.

Susan Sinnott, *Zebulon Pike.* Chicago: Childrens, 1990. A solid biography of one of the first American explorers of the Louisiana Territory. Illustrations, some in color, complement the text; a bibliography is included.

R. Conrad Stein, *Francisco de Coronado.* Chicago: Childrens, 1992. Traces the sixteenth-century journey of Coronado from Mexico City into the Great Plains. Illustrations, maps, and a bibliography add to the text.

Internet Sources

History Buff's Home Page, "Press Coverage of the Louisiana Purchase Articles," 1999. www.historybuff.com/library/reflp.html. Reproduces half a dozen newspaper accounts, appearing between March 16 and November 30, 1803, and taken from the *Boston Columbian Centinel* and the *Massachusetts Federalist*. These articles cover the negotiations for and approval of the Louisiana Purchase Treaty.

National Archives and Records Administration, "The Louisiana Purchase," 1996. www.nara.gov/exhall/originals/louistxt.html. Reproduces the entire text of the Louisiana Purchase Treaty as well as the two accompanying conventions that spell out the financial arrangements for paying for the territory.

Alamo de Paras, "The Louisiana Purchase of 1803," 1999. www.flash.net/~alamo3/archives/documents/louistxt.htm. Provides useful links to such documents as the Treaty of San Ildefonso, transferring Louisiana from Spain to France; congressional authorization for President Thomas Jefferson to take possession of the territory; and U.S. plans for governing the new possession.

Works Consulted

Books

Thomas Perkins Abernethy, *The Burr Conspiracy*. New York: Oxford University Press, 1954. A carefully researched examination of Aaron Burr's attempt to use Louisiana border disputes between Spain and the United States to seize Spanish territory.

Stephen E. Ambrose, *Undaunted Courage: Meriwether Lewis, Thomas Jefferson, and the Opening of the American West*. New York: Simon and Schuster, 1996. A thorough, readable account of the Lewis and Clark expedition, detailing its organization, travels, and final outcome. Illustrations and maps enhance the text.

Jean-Bernard Bossu, *Travels in the Interior of North America, 1751–1762*. Trans. and ed. Seymour Feiler. Norman: University of Oklahoma Press, 1962. Memoir recounting the adventures of a French naval officer in Louisiana in the 1750s.

Henry Marie Brackenridge, *Views of Louisiana Together with a Journal of a Voyage up the Missouri River in 1811*. Chicago: Quadrangle Books, 1814. Based on firsthand experience, the writer describes the land, wildlife, and inhabitants found along the Missouri River not long after the Louisiana Purchase.

T. H. Breen, ed., *The Power of Words: Documents in American History*. Vol. 1. To 1877. New York: HarperCollinsCollege, 1996. Reprints a number of letters concerned with the Louisiana Purchase. Of particular interest are those by Thomas Jefferson on the constitutionality of the acquisition.

Gerhard Casper, *Separating Power: Essays on the Founding Period*. Cambridge, MA: Harvard University Press, 1997. Devotes one section to the constitutional issues involved in the Louisiana Purchase.

Michael Coe, Dean Snow, and Elizabeth Benson, *Atlas of Ancient America*. New York: Facts On File, 1986. Filled with illustrations and maps, the sections on the Mississippian culture and the Great Plains dwellers are packed with useful information.

Isaac Cox, ed., *The Journeys of René Robert Cavelier, Sieur de la Salle*. Vol. 1. Austin, TX: Pemberton, 1968. Eyewitness accounts of La Salle's 1682 voyage down the Mississippi River.

David Brion Davis and Steven Mintz, eds., *The Boisterous Sea of Liberty: A Documentary History of America from Discovery Through the Civil War*. New York: Oxford University Press, 1998. Reprints a number of letters concerning the Louisiana Purchase.

Alexander DeConde, *This Affair of Louisiana*. New York: Scribner's, 1976. A well-researched study of the factors, particularly the American drive to expand west, that led to the Louisiana Purchase. The text is complemented by an extensive bibliographical essay.

Documents Pertaining to the Purchase and Exploration of Louisiana. Boston: Houghton, Mifflin, 1904. Reprints an essay by Thomas Jefferson on the borders of Louisiana and an account of the 1804 journey down the Red River by William Dunbar.

David Ewing Duncan, *Hernando de Soto: A Savage Conquest in the Americas.* New York: Crown, 1995. An excellent and exhaustive biography of this Spanish conquistador, with much detail about his adventures exploring the Mississippi and beyond.

John E. Findling and Frank W. Thackeray, eds., *Events That Changed America in the Nineteenth Century.* Westport, CT: Greenwood, 1997. The essay on the Louisiana Purchase gives a brief but full description of the history of the territory after the sale.

Dan L. Flores, ed., *Jefferson and Southwestern Exploration: The Freeman and Custis Accounts of the Red River Expedition of 1806.* Norman: University of Oklahoma Press, 1984. A reprint of Freeman and Custis's accounts of their 1806 expedition along the Red River.

James K. Hosmer, *The History of the Louisiana Purchase.* New York: D. Appleton, 1902. A thorough study that examines the history of Louisiana and its sale from the French viewpoint.

Louis Houck, *The Boundaries of the Louisiana Purchase.* New York: Arno, 1901. Details the establishing of the borders of the Louisiana Territory.

James Q. Howard, *History of the Louisiana Purchase.* Chicago: Callaghan, 1902. Published for the centennial of the Louisiana Purchase, this brief study is filled with extensive primary quotations.

Fred L. Israel, ed., *Major Presidential Decisions.* New York: Chelsea House, 1980. Reprints almost a hundred documents written by Jefferson, Livingston, Madison, Monroe, and others involved in the Louisiana Purchase.

Meriwether Lewis and William Clark, *The Journals of Lewis and Clark.* Ed. Frank Bergon. New York: Penguin Books, 1989. An excellent one-volume selection of entries from the journals kept by Lewis and Clark during their exploration.

E. Wilson Lyon, *Louisiana in French Diplomacy: 1759–1804.* Norman: University of Oklahoma Press, 1934. An exacting, scholarly work describing the importance of Louisiana to French diplomatic efforts from the French and Indian War to the territory's sale.

———, *The Man Who Sold Louisiana. The Career of Francois Barbe-Marbois.* Norman: University of Oklahoma Press, 1942. A biography of the minister of the public treasury, who was the French negotiator for the Louisiana Purchase Treaty.

Robert Meredith and E. Brooks Smith, eds., *Exploring the Great River: Early Voyages on the Mississippi from De Soto to La Salle*. Boston: Little, Brown, 1969. A collection of excerpts from journals and memoirs of those involved in early European exploration of the Mississippi.

Zebulon Pike, *Zebulon Pike's Arkansas Journal: In Search of the Southern Louisiana Purchase Boundary Line*. Ed. Stephen Harding Hart and Archer Butler Hulbert. Westport, CT: Greenwood, 1932. Pike's journal of his 1806 Louisiana expedition.

Perry T. Rathbone, *Westward the Way: The Character and Development of the Louisiana Purchase as Seen by Artists and Writers of the Nineteenth Century*. St. Louis: City Art Museum of St. Louis, 1954. Filled with original paintings from the period 1803–1860, this collection of essays looks at various aspects of the Louisiana Territory, such as its wildlife, its Native American residents, and its American settlements.

Robert V. Remini, *The Battle of New Orleans*. New York: Viking, 1999. A good, brief study of this important engagement, written by a noted authority on Andrew Jackson and his time.

James Roberts, *The Narrative of James Roberts: Soldier in the Revolutionary War and at the Battle of New Orleans*. Hattiesburg, MS: Book Farm, 1858. An interesting account by a participant of the battle for New Orleans.

Marshall Sprague, *So Vast So Beautiful a Land: Louisiana and the Purchase*. Boston: Little, Brown, 1974. A scholarly examination of Louisiana and its sale, with particular emphasis on the character of those involved in exploration, settlement, and purchase. Maps and illustrations pepper the book.

Robert M. Utley, *A Life Wild and Perilous: Mountain Men and the Paths to the Pacific*. New York: Holt, 1997. Biographical sketches of the mountain men who were the first Americans to enter much of the Louisiana Territory.

Dale Van Every, *The Final Challenge: The American Frontier, 1804–1845*. New York: Morrow, 1964. The first part of this examination deals with the early American exploration of the Louisiana Territory.

F. Adolph Wislizenus, *A Journey to the Rocky Mountains in the Year 1839*. Trans. Francis A. Wislizenus. St. Louis: Missouri Historical Society, 1912. Written by a German doctor who made an 1839 crossing of the Great Plains to the Rocky Mountains.

Internet Sources

Americanrevolution.org, "Spanish Covert Aid," 1999. www.americanrevolution.org/secret.html. Provides the full translated text of the 1776 royal order commanding the governor of Spanish Louisiana to aid the rebelling English colonists in the Revolutionary War.

The Avalon Project, "Treaty of Friendship, Limits, and Navigation Between Spain and the United States:

October 27, 1795," 1998. www.yale. edu/lawweb/avalon/diplomacy/ sp1795.htm. Reproduces the entire text of the 1795 document, known as either the Treaty of San Lorenzo or Pinckney's Treaty.

———, "Treaty of San Ildefonso: October 1, 1800," 1997. www.yale.edu/ lawweb/ avalon/ildefens.htm. Gives the complete translated text of the treaty, in which Spain agreed to return Louisiana to France.

Index

Picture Credits

Cover Photo: © Bettmann/Corbis

Archive Photos, 22, 27, 38, 47, 50, 53, 60, 63, 70, 84

Culver Pictures, 71

Dover Publications, Incorporated, 80 (both)

Library of Congress, 11, 15, 18, 23, 25, 30, 32, 45, 55, 56, 66, 79, 86, 87, 90, 94, 95

Missouri Historical Society, 73

Montana Historical Society, 82

North Wind Picture Archives, 13, 33, 41, 42, 93

Oregon Historical Society, 81

Prints Old and Rare, 88

Public Domain, 92

Stock Montage, 21, 28, 58

U.S. Fish & Wildlife Service, 12

About the Author

James A. Corrick has been a professional writer and editor for twenty years and is the author of twenty books as well as two hundred articles and short stories. His other books for Lucent include *The Early Middle Ages, The Late Middle Ages, The Battle of Gettysburg, The Byzantine Empire, The Renaissance, The Industrial Revolution,* and *The Civil War: Life Among the Soldiers and Cavalry.* Along with a Ph.D. in English, Corrick's academic background includes a graduate degree in the biological sciences. He has taught English, tutored minority students, edited magazines for the National Space Society, been a science writer for the Muscular Dystrophy Association, and edited and indexed books on history, economics, and literature for Columbia University Press, MIT Press, and others. He and his wife live in Tucson, Arizona, and when not writing, he reads, swims, walks, frequents bookstores, and holds forth on any number of topics.

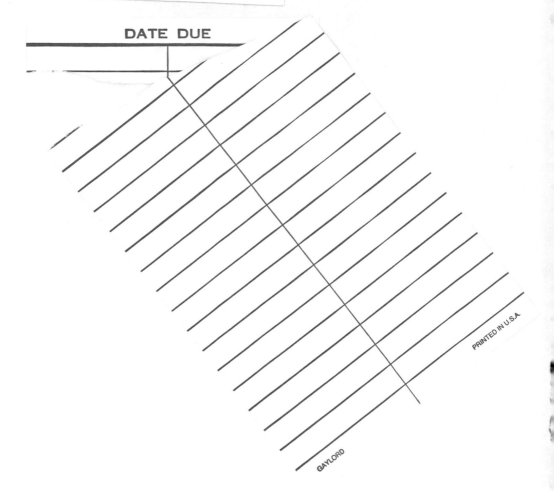

DATE DUE

GAYLORD

PRINTED IN U.S.A.